MW00639153

THIS BOOK BELONGS TO

_____

Daily Declarations OF Faith

FOR WOMEN

BroadStreet
PUBLISHING

BroadStreet Publishing® Group, LLC
Savage, Minnesota, USA
BroadStreetPublishing.com

Daily Declarations OF *Faith* FOR WOMEN

ISBN-13: 978-1-4245-5205-4 (flexi-faux)
ISBN-13: 978-1-4245-5206-1 (e-book)

Disclaimer: This book is a resource for daily encouragement, hope, and prayer because we believe that Jesus Christ's "divine power has given to us all things that pertain to life and godliness" (2 Peter 1:3). The author and publisher do not claim to treat or diagnose any condition and are not responsible for results from these declarations. The information in this book is not a substitute for professional advice or treatment.

Cover and interior design by Chris Garborg at garborgdesign.com
Typesetting by Kjell Garborg at garborgdesign.com

Printed in China
18 19 20   5 4 3

CONTENTS

· · · · · · · · · · · · ·

INTRODUCTION

Inside of every born again believer is an insatiable hunger to draw close and then closer to God. There is only one way to accomplish this heavenly desire within us, and it is to read the Word of God, meditate on it, and then declare it at all times!

Discovering afresh His wonderful promises and then declaring them out loud can renew our faith. We've chosen a theme to declare each month—*the Word, faith, fruitfulness, the name of Jesus, blessing, love, freedom from fear, strength, healing, the Holy Spirit, praise,* and *salvation!*

What do you do when it's March where you're declaring the truths about fruitfulness and you need freedom from fear? Jump over to the Scriptures and declarations in July. See what happens as you meditate on and declare God's powerful Word. Read each day's Scripture several times during the day until the Word of God sticks to your ribs and gets into your heart! And declare it out loud so you can hear it: So then faith

comes by hearing, and hearing by the Word of God (see Romans 10:17).

You may even want to get your Bible out and read several verses before and after the selection so that the whole meaning of the Scripture will come alive in your spirit! Or try reading all the declarations for that month every day!

It's an extra blessing to see family unity strengthened by declaring and reading God's Word together. Fussing, complaining, and arguing turns to praising and loving God and each other in Jesus' name! This is one of the most powerful things that has ever happened in our lives—let it happen in yours!

The time you dedicate to the Word of God will be the most valuable time you have ever spent! I believe your spirit will soar because the amazing love of God that will come forth with power and truth. Each Scripture was selected to inspire you into a higher plane of love for Jesus, and the declarations provide a way for you to go directly into the very presence of God.

Joan Hunter

joanhunter.org

JANUARY

The Word

In the beginning God created
the heavens and the earth.

GENESIS 1:1

God took nothing and from nothing He created the universe. How did He create it? From Hebrews 11:3, we get the important clue which can unlock the entire Bible to you in a totally new and different way: By faith, we understand that the worlds were framed by the Word of God, so that the things which are seen were not made of things which are visible.

It is by the Word of God, not by the hands of God nor by the feet of God, mind of God, or power of God. The Word of God frames our faith. We can create a whole new world for ourselves by speaking the Word of God for our lives!

It's one thing to read the Word of God, but it's another thing to memorize the Word of God. Get the Word of God in you. Possess it and declare, "It's mine. It's mine. It's mine! I take it for myself!"

The Sword of the Word

> For the word of God is living and active,
> sharper than any two-edged sword,
> piercing to the division of soul and of
> spirit, of joints and of marrow, and
> discerning the thoughts and intentions of
> the heart.
>
> HEBREWS 4:12, ESV

Father, nothing can withstand the sword of your Word, which is mightier and more forceful than all the nuclear power in this world. With that sword in my hand each and every day, there's nothing I can't overcome. I'm a winner, not a loser, because your Word has made it so. I delight and revel in the power of your wonderful Word, which cleanses my heart, lifts my thoughts heavenward and is like an invincible two-edged sword preparing the way. It's quick, too, because it doesn't take long to hit the target.

The Mind of Christ

For "who has known the mind of the LORD that he may instruct Him?" But we have the mind of Christ.

1 CORINTHIANS 2:16

Father, what a privilege it is to know that I'm not operating with a natural mind. I praise you that my thoughts are heavenly because I have the mind of Christ! I thank you that I don't have to worry about the silly things that come into my mind every once in a while, because when they start, I can just relax and realize that I have the mind of Christ. I don't have to hang on to the garbage and worries of the world, but instead, I'm concentrating on my eternal destination. I thank you, Father, and praise you for that!

It Accomplishes All

So shall My word be that goes forth from
   My mouth;
It shall not return to Me void,
But it shall accomplish what I please,
And it shall prosper in the thing for
   which I sent it.

ISAIAH 55:11

Father, I thank you that your Word does everything—all that you say it will do. I thank you that it accomplishes exactly what you say, without any ifs, ands or buts. I thank you for the knowledge that your Word never says anything that will fall by the wayside and die. I praise you because you've said it never returns to you void. Your Word grows, multiplies, thrives, flourishes, and blooms wherever and whenever you send it. I praise you that it never dies on the vine but is constantly growing and multiplying!

Hidden in My Heart

Jesus replied, "But even more blessed are
all who hear the word of God and put it
into practice."

LUKE 11:28

Father, I bless you because I am blessed! I have
heard your Word, and I keep it hidden in my heart that
I might not sin against you. I thank you that because
I keep your Word, I am blessed in everything I do. I
thank you that I have had the opportunity to hear your
Word. Father, I am blessed among all the people of
every nation in the world because I have the ability
to hear your Word. I thank you for your Word, which
permeates my entire being and blesses me as I read,
memorize, and declare it! Father, I am keeping it in my
heart forever, and I love you for giving your Word!

Walking in Righteousness

All Scripture is inspired by God and
profitable for teaching, for reproof, for
correction, for training in righteousness.

2 TIMOTHY 3:16, NASB

Father, I praise you that there is no guesswork with
Scripture. I thank you for the knowledge that you
inspired every word, and you had many purposes
in inspiring those men of old to write down your
thoughts because it establishes truth and godly
principles for us to live by. I praise you, Father, that
your Word has power to rebuke, admonish, and
censure us. When I get out of line, your Word is right
there to correct me and help me straighten out again.
Thank you for giving me instructions on how to live
in the beauty of your righteousness! I'm walking in
righteousness today!

Everlasting Word

Heaven and earth will pass away,
but My words will by no means pass away.

MARK 13:31

Father, how I praise you because your Word will never pass away. Friends are transient. Possessions are subject to change. But your Word cannot! Even when everything else fades away or goes down the drain, your words shall remain forever and forever. Even though we come into this world in a perishable container, which we know won't last forever, you have given us something to put into our temporary housing that will last eternally: your Word! Thank you, Father. When the storms of life are thundering around me and it looks as though everything may fall apart, I stand on the secure knowledge that your words shall never pass away!

JANUARY 7

Heavenly Bread

And Jesus answered him, "It is written,
'Man shall not live by bread alone.'"

LUKE 4:4, ESV

I praise you, Father, for the spiritual banquet you've given me in your Word. I feast every day on this manna, and my body thrives on the heavenly vitamins you provide. I thank you that I do not have to live by physical things alone, but I can find spiritual health in your Word, which assures me of a healthy body, a sound mind, and an endless supply of enthusiasm for tackling the tasks you put before me each day. Jesus, you are the Bread of Life! Thank you for making each and every word in Scripture count in my life. I love you for that!

Abide in Me

> If you abide in me, and my words abide in you, ask whatever you wish, and it will be done for you.
>
> JOHN 15:7, NIV

Father, I love the word *abide*. I praise you that as long as I dwell, reside, live, submit, and let your words snuggle down deep inside of me, you have given me the awesome privilege of asking whatever I will. I rest safely and securely in the knowledge that what I ask will be done for me. You simply gave me those two little conditions—that I abide in you and let your words abide in me—for those blessings of Abraham to overtake and overcome me. So I do that, Father. Come abide in me and I abide in you. You are a generous God who promises me every good thing.

God of Action

"I am ready to perform My word."

JEREMIAH 1:12

Father, you lose no time performing your Word. I can see you in my mind speeding up and expediting all the things you've promised because you are not a God who sits back and does nothing, but you are a God of action! I thank you that you make short work of those things, which stand in the way of the performance of your Word. Father, you don't use delaying tactics like the devil, but you are prompt and right on schedule at all times in fulfilling your Word!

A Weapon to the World

> I have hidden your word in my heart that
> I might not sin against you. ... Your word,
> LORD, is eternal; it stands firm in the
> heavens.
>
> PSALM 119:11, 89, NIV

Father, thank you for letting me hide your wonderful, brilliant, resplendent, dazzling, glorious words in my heart for the purpose of having them there to remind me not to sin. Your words are so sharp and penetrating; they can go through the greatest temptation that might ever come my way to protect me from the fiery darts of the devil himself. I praise you for that weapon with which to protect myself at all times from sin. And how I thank you, Father, that we have no arguing and debating about your Word because it has been settled in heaven for eternity! I live by your heaven-made rules and don't have to depend on the peculiarities of humans to live by! I love your Word.

A Glorious Light

> Your word is a lamp to my feet
> and a light to my path.
>
> PSALM 119:105, ESV

Father, I thank you that I'm not stumbling around in the dark wondering which way to go. You have put your Word unto my feet so that I may receive understanding and enlightenment to my mind, my heart, and my soul! Father, I love your law, and I meditate in it day and night because of the glorious light it sheds abroad. I thank you that the path on which I walk is one where I have no fear that I might fall down in the darkness. My path is flooded with light with no hiding places for sin to lurk and get me. Thank you that your light is brighter than any light of this world, and it's turned right onto my path!

Love Broke Through

The teaching of your word gives light, so
even the simple can understand.

PSALM 119:130, NLT

    Father, I thank you that your Word broke through
the cold, stony heart I once had. I praise you that
when one single word sneaked through that crevice
in my sinful armor, it began to give light to my life.
Thank you that the unfolding of your Word gave me
understanding, discernment, and comprehension. I
long for your words to give me more and more light.
Be merciful to me, show me your favor, establish my
steps, and direct them by means of your Word! I love
your Word, so I'll keep on hearing, receiving, loving,
and obeying!

More than Silver and Gold

The law from your mouth is more precious
to me than thousands of pieces of silver
and gold.

PSALM 119:72, NIV

Father, I bless you that the world can have its silver
and gold with its fluctuating prices, but your Word
stands above all of the treasures of this world and
never changes. I praise you because your promise
surpasses anything this world has to offer. Thank you
that it is better than silver and gold, houses and lands,
or any other kind of material possessions. I thank you
that the entrance of your Word illumines my entire
life and teaches me wise and right discernment, good
judgment and knowledge, and the Earth is full of your
loving kindness and mercy.

JANUARY 14

A Solid Rock

Therefore everyone who hears these
words of mine and puts them into
practice is like a wise man who built his
house on the rock. The rain came down,
the streams rose, and the winds blew and
beat against that house; yet it did not fall,
because it had its foundation on the rock.

MATTHEW 7:24-25, NIV

Father, I praise you that my house is built upon a
rock because I have heard your Word, and I am a doer
of the Word and not just a hearer. Because of this,
you have called me a wise and productive woman,
who is practical in her ways. I bless you, Father, for
the promise of your Word, which says that when the
rains fell and the floods overflowed, and even when
the winds became hurricane force and beat upon my
house, it didn't fall because it was founded on a rock.
My house will continue to stand on that solid rock!

JANUARY 15

Come Alive

It is the Spirit who gives life; the flesh profits nothing. The words that I speak to you are spirit, and they are life.

JOHN 6:63

Father, I praise you that the Holy Spirit quickens your Word. I thank you that the Spirit is the Life-giver because there is no profit in the flesh. I thank you that the words you have spoken and recorded in your Word give me spirit and life. I bless you, Father, that I am not dead in the trespasses of sin and disaster, but I am alive because my spirit has been quickened, energized, and made alive by your words!

Overcome the World

> You are of God, little children, and have
> overcome them, because He who is in you
> is greater than he who is in the world.
>
> 1 JOHN 4:4

Father, how I applaud and glorify your Word. I thank you for the magnificent promises in your Word. I thank you that your Son, Jesus Christ, lives in me, and He is greater and mightier than the devil and all his doings. I don't have to submit to his torment any longer because I know that I know that I know that what your Word tells me is true. You have said that there is a greater One living in me than is living in the world, and I believe, receive, declare, and possess this promise for myself! I thank you that regardless of how big the devil might look to me in certain situations, I can stand tall and look down on him, knowing that I have far more power than he does!

JANUARY 17

Provision for Success

This Book of the Law shall not depart from
your mouth, but you shall meditate in it
day and night, that you may observe to
do according to all that is written in it. For
then you will make your way prosperous,
and then you will have good success.

JOSHUA 1:8

Your Word is in my mouth, Father, and I'm not taking
it out! For too many years, I had the filth of the devil
coming out, and I like what you've given me. I praise
you that I am made righteous and am in right standing
with you because of your saving grace. I thank you
that because I am walking according to your Word, I
am prospering and am having good success. I praise
you, Father, that I don't have to depend on the world
for instructions on how to be successful. I can depend
on your Word because you don't make provision
for failure; you only make provision for success! I'm
prospering! I'm successful! I'm blessed because you
said so!

Walking in Life

There is therefore now no condemnation to those who are in Christ Jesus, who do not walk according to the flesh, but according to the Spirit.

ROMANS 8:1

Father, I thank you that I walk in victory today and *every* day because the blood of the Lamb has redeemed me. I'm washed clean inside and out because the best detergent in the whole world is your precious blood. Therefore, I have no condemnation or guilt in my life because my sins are washed away *forever!* Father, I'm not interested in walking after the flesh, because that leads to death, but I'm walking after the law of the Spirit of life, which is the law of my new being, and it has freed me from the law of sin and death. Hallelujah! I'm not only walking, but I'm dancing in the newness of life!

For Us

> What then shall we say to these things? If
> God is for us, who can be against us.
>
> ROMANS 8:31

Father, I praise and glorify you because *you are for me*! Together, you and I make a majority, and nothing and no one can stand against us. Father, by myself, I might not be so super, but with you, I'm a majority at all times. I thank you that I don't have to rely on my own strength, but I'm walking in your power and might. Together we can move mountains. Hallelujah! I'm victorious because you're on my side. The devil can't win against me. His demons can't win against me. You could make it without me, but I sure can't do it without you!

Not the Same

> Therefore, if anyone is in Christ, he is a
> new creation. The old has passed away;
> behold, the new has come.
>
> 2 CORINTHIANS 5:17, ESV

Father, I praise you that I am in Christ because I have been born again of the incorruptible seed that can't be contaminated, spoiled, or tainted! I thank you that I am a *new* creature. I praise you that the individual who was me no longer exists. I praise you that all of the things of my old nature have passed away, and I'm a brand new creature in Christ. I praise you that everything about me has changed and that all things are *new*! I praise you that the month of January always ushers in a new year, and it reminds me of the newness of life in Christ Jesus. I praise you for making me and keeping me *new*!

JANUARY 21

Beautiful Image

Don't lie to each other, for you have stripped off your old sinful nature and all its wicked deeds. Put on your new nature, and be renewed as you learn to know your Creator and become like him.

COLOSSIANS 3:9-10, NLT

Glory to God, I'm a new creation! Father, I praise you for making the Christian life so simple, because you so beautifully tell us what to do and what not to do. I have put off the old with all my evil ways, and have put on the new. I like the new me better! I thank you that my mind is renewed and is no longer conformed to this world because I have been created in your beautiful image. I love you, Father, and praise you for loving me so much that you put all these beautiful promises in your Word!

A New Covenant

"Behold, the days are coming, declares the Lord, when I will establish a new covenant with the house of Israel and with the house of Judah." ... "For this is the covenant that I will make with the house of Israel after those days, declares the Lord: I will put my laws into their minds, and write them on their hearts, and I will be their God, and they shall be my people."

HEBREWS 8:8,10, ESV

Father, I praise you and thank you for the new covenant, which you have given to us. You have written and imprinted your laws upon my innermost thoughts and understanding, and you have forever engraved them in my heart. I praise you for the way you have inscribed all of these laws permanently upon my heart, so wherever I go, I can never get away from you. Hallelujah! I'm a person of your new covenant!

Walk in Love

And now I plead with you, lady, not as
though I wrote a new commandment to
you, but that which we have had from the
beginning: that we love one another.

2 JOHN 5

Father, how I praise you that you instruct us to live
the love-life and walk the love-life. I'm going to walk
and talk the love-life at all times and love the unlovely.
I praise you for the power you give me to walk this
love-walk and for the instructions you give me. Father,
let this year become the most loving of my life. I praise
you for giving me a special infilling of your precious
love.

A New Name

He who has an ear, let him hear what the Spirit says to the churches. To him who overcomes I will give some of the hidden manna to eat. And I will give him a white stone, and on the stone a new name written which no one knows except him who receives it.

REVELATION 2:17

Father, I praise you for my ears that hear the Spirit. I thank you for letting me be an overcomer in all things through Christ who strengthens me. I praise you that some day soon I will eat of the hidden manna and will have a brand new name written in stone—a name that is just for me. Father, I praise you for your goodness to me. I love you because I don't have to look at things that are temporal because they are subject to change. I look at those things that are eternal and lasting. Hallelujah! My ears are hearing, and I'm overcoming.

God's Child

And he who was seated on the throne said, "Behold, I am making all things new." Also he said, "Write this down, for these words are trustworthy and true." And he said to me, "It is done! I am the Alpha and the Omega, the beginning and the end. To the thirsty I will give from the spring of the water of life without payment. The one who conquers will have this heritage, and I will be his God and he will be my son.

REVELATION 21:5-7, ESV

Jesus, you are the beginning and the end! Your words are true and faithful! You make all things, including me, brand new! When I was thirsty, you freely gave to me the water of life. I thank you for the power of the Holy Spirit; I am an overcomer at all times, and because of this, I shall inherit all things. God, you are my God, and Jesus, your redemptive work at Calvary made me God's child. Hallelujah!

A New Year

Knowing this, that our old man was crucified with Him, that the body of sin might be done away with, that we should no longer be slaves of sin. For he who has died has been freed from sin.

ROMANS 6:6-7

Father, how I thank you that with this *new* year, because of my *new* life, my *old* self is crucified and lifeless. I don't have to walk under sin's power and dominion any longer. I praise you that the old, unregenerate, unrenewed self is dead, dead, dead! Therefore, I don't have to serve sin any longer. Sin is no longer my master. When I learned to die to self, you freed me from sin, wickedness, impurity, iniquity, and error. I am now a servant to a new Master who has revitalized me in the newness of Christ!

A Precious Spirit

Jesus answered, "Most assuredly, I say to you, unless one is born of water and the Spirit, he cannot enter the kingdom of God. That which is born of the flesh is flesh, and that which is born of the Spirit is spirit."

JOHN 3:5-6

Father, I praise you that I am living in newness of life because I have been born again by your precious Spirit. I thank you that I am no longer a fleshly creature, subject to the things of this world, but because I have been born again, I am a spirit-being under your control. I praise you that you provided such a beautiful and simple way for me to have eternal life! I'm walking toward the kingdom of God with a lift in my walk because I'm a new creation!

Perfect Will of God

Do not conform to the pattern of this
world, but be transformed by the
renewing of your mind. Then you will be
able to test and approve what God's will
is—his good, pleasing and perfect will.

ROMANS 12:2, NIV

Father, I thank you that in my new life I do not have
to be conformed to this world. I don't have to dress
the way they do. I don't have to act the way the world
acts, and I don't have to talk the way the world does.
My new life gives me freedom to live the way you
want me to. I thank you that my mind is renewed with
new ideas, ideals, and attitudes. Father, I present my
body and all its members to you as a living sacrifice
because it is my reasonable and intelligent service to
you. I praise you and thank you for your grace, which
made this all possible. I shall glory in you forever! How
perfect are your ways! They are faultless, spotless, and
unblemished!

Overcomer

Being confident of this very thing, that He who has begun a good work in you will complete it until the day of Jesus Christ.

PHILIPPIANS 1:6

Father, I praise you for confidence in my new life. Even though I can't always see the end of what you have planned for me, I have the complete knowledge and faith that you will keep working in me until the day of Jesus Christ. I praise you, Father, because I don't have to worry. You have promised it in your Word! You're still working in me and because of this, I'm an overcomer confident that whatever is born of you overcomes the whole world. So I'm going to shout, "I'm an overcomer! I'm an overcomer because God is working in me!"

Fully Believe

But now he has reconciled you by Christ's
physical body through death to present
you holy in his sight, without blemish and
free from accusation— if you continue in
your faith, established and firm, and do
not move from the hope held out in the
gospel. This is the gospel that you heard
and that has been proclaimed to every
creature under heaven, and of which I,
Paul, have become a servant.

COLOSSIANS 1:22-23, NIV

Father, how I praise you that I stand before you
as a new creation because you have buried my sins
in the deepest sea never to be remembered again!
How I praise you for this. You said the only condition
was that I fully believe the truth and stand in it firmly.
Father, I do, I do, I do! You are the truth and I stand in
the hope of the gospel. I'm standing tall and straight
and can look the world straight in the eye because my
sins are gone, gone, gone!

Total Victory

And we know that all things work
together for good to those who love God,
to those who are the called according to
His purpose.

ROMANS 8:28

Everything, everything, *everything* that happens to
me works together for my own good. I thank you that
you can take the biggest mess and turn everything in it
around so that it turns out for my good. Regardless of
how dark and gloomy things look, I know it's working
for my good. I praise you that when I call for help,
the very tide of the battle turns and my enemies flee,
all because of you! Thank you that you take any old
mess and make a miracle out of it! Thank you, Father,
for a month of total victory because I have stood on
your promises. Thank you for the extra prosperity
that has come into my house; thank you for the health
you have given me; thank you for showing me that
miracles and wonders still happen today. Thank you
for the marvelous victory you have given me simply by
declaring your promises and the truth of your Word.

FEBRUARY

Faith

The Christian life is so simple because we only have to do two things:

1. Do what God tells us to do.
2. Stop doing what He tells us not to do.

And how do we do what God wants us to do? The psalmist tells us: *"Your word I have hidden in my heart, that I might not sin against You"* (119:11).

Once you establish in your own mind that the Bible is the actual spoken Word of God written down for posterity, your faith can begin that upward climb as you read, declare, memorize, and hide the Word in your heart.

How do you increase your faith? *"Faith comes by hearing, and hearing by the word of God"* (Romans 10:17). We need to *hear* the Word of God.

How can we hear the Word of God? By reading the Bible. The Bible is God's personal love letter to you, and if you will just read it, believe it, declare it, and live it, then every promise in the Word is yours!

FEBRUARY 1

Faith: A Pledge

Now faith is the substance of things hoped
for, the evidence of things not seen.

HEBREWS 11:1

Thank you, Father, that faith is the pledge and the
confirmation of the things I long and hope for, but
which I can't see at the moment. Even though I don't
see some things with my natural eyes, in my spirit I
can see them as a reality. Because of this, I can see
what is not revealed to my senses. Father, I thank you
for Noah, who had never heard of rain, but because
he was prompted by faith, he diligently constructed
and prepared an ark through the eyes of faith. In the
same way I can also look with my eyes of faith and
see things come to pass which were just a hope in the
past! Hallelujah!

Faith: A Gift

> But without faith it is impossible to please Him, for he who comes to God must believe that He is, and that He is a rewarder of those who diligently seek Him.
>
> HEBREWS 11:6

Father, thank you for making it so plain that if I don't use the faith you've given me, there is no way I can please you. I don't have to work up something on my own because your faith is a gift. I believe in you and I believe that you are the God of all gods! I believe that you are a rewarder of those who diligently seek you. I will continue to diligently seek you, and I thank you for rewarding my faith. You've made your promises so easy for me to accept through faith! I am receiving those rewards right now!

Shield of Faith

In all circumstances take up the shield of faith, with which you can extinguish all the flaming darts of the evil one.

EPHESIANS 6:16, ESV

Thank you, Father, for surrounding me with your shield of faith so that I am completely protected from every kind of wickedness. Any kind of wicked temptation, insult, accusation, or attack is quenched and conquered by the shield of faith that I wear constantly, and not even the devil himself can get through it! I walk in the world and I am not afraid. Nothing can harm me. I walk in faith! I talk in faith! I pray in faith, and I rejoice in faith! Father, you are my strength and my fortress, and I praise you because with my shield of faith, I live in victory every minute of the day, every day of the year!

Unique Faith

For by the grace given me I say to every one of you: Do not think of yourself more highly than you ought, but rather think of yourself with sober judgment, in accordance with the faith God has distributed to each of you.

ROMANS 12:3, NIV

Father, I thank you that you have given to me the measure of faith I need to be exactly the kind of person you want me to be, and to do all the things you want me to do! We are all different and distinct individuals, and yet you have given to each of us the same measure of faith as everyone else, so that I can take on the unique tasks that fit in your perfect plan for me. I thank you that you have given me just as much faith as anyone else in the world because all your children are precious to you. I'm using and developing my measure of faith daily!

Every Good Thing

I pray that the sharing of your faith may become effective for the full knowledge of every good thing that is in us for the sake of Christ.

PHILEMON 6

My faith produces good fruit in me! It produces and promotes full recognition, appreciation, understanding, and precise knowledge. I identify myself with the ever-truthful God who cannot deceive, and my faith grows, multiplies, and abounds! I praise you for a sound mind; for the salvation of my family; for health, wealth, and happiness; for joy, love, peace, prosperity, and abundance. I praise you for every good thing! Hallelujah!

FEBRUARY 6

All Things Possible

I can do all things through Christ who
strengthens me.

PHILIPPIANS 4:13

Thank you for the faith to know that I am
empowered through Jesus Christ to do *all things*! I
can handle any situation because Jesus strengthens
and equips me to succeed in even the most difficult
situations and problems that I face. Through Christ,
every obstacle has become a stepping-stone for
me, every problem an opportunity. Through Christ,
I have the willpower to overcome any and all of my
bad habits. I thank you because your Word doesn't
say I can only do some things through Christ which
strengthens me, but it says *I can do all things*!
Hallelujah, that's power! I thank you that I can live
in divine health! I thank you because I can live in
prosperity. I thank you that I can live in total victory!

Live by Faith

Now the just shall live by faith; but if
anyone draws back, My soul has no
pleasure in him.

HEBREWS 10:38

Glory to God, I'm living by faith! I live by the
confident conviction that you are God and I am your
beloved child. I believe in you, cling to you, and trust
in you, and because of this, I can rely wholly and
continually on you through Jesus Christ! I bless you
for the warning that if I draw back, you will have no
pleasure in me. Father, I'm living in faith, walking in
faith, talking in faith, and running in faith because I
want to please you!

Fullness of Faith

For by grace you have been saved through faith, and that not of yourselves; it is the gift of God.

EPHESIANS 2:8

I don't have to save myself! Hallelujah! I thank you, Father, that I didn't do a thing to deserve your unmerited favor, but because of your grace, I have been delivered from judgment and made a partaker of Christ's salvation. I thank you that it was a beautiful gift that you just gave to me, not something that I accomplished by my works or striving. Salvation is mine because you loved me so much that you sent your Son to save me from perishing in the darkness of sin and death. I thank you for the gift of everlasting life I have in Christ. Because you have shown me the fullness of your love, I love you, Father! I love your Son, Jesus Christ! I love the new life you have given me through your beloved Son!

FEBRUARY 9

Saints of the Light

Giving thanks to the Father who has qualified us to be partakers of the inheritance of the saints in the light. He has delivered us from the power of darkness and conveyed us into the kingdom of the Son of His love.

COLOSSIANS 1:12-13

I will thank you and praise you forever, Father, because I am delivered! I've been taken out of the control and the dominion of darkness, changed so that I am qualified to share the inheritance of the saints, and translated into the kingdom of light! Glorious Father, how I praise you that because of your loving kindness and mercy, I have been made a partaker of the inheritance of all the saints! I've been delivered from bad habits, evil thoughts, and delivered from the very power of the devil! I want to say *thank you, thank you, thank you* because you have reached inside of me and turned me into a brand new person, and you have sent me straight into the kingdom of your beloved Son, Jesus Christ!

Rejoicing Day by Day

Rejoice in the Lord always.
Again I will say, rejoice!

PHILIPPIANS 4:4

I have so many wonderful reasons to rejoice in you, Father. I rejoice in your presence in my life! I rejoice in each new day you give me to live, to love, to enjoy, and to help others! I rejoice that I am your child and that you love me more than I love myself. I rejoice in your Word, in your power, and in your glory! I rejoice in the blessings you shower upon me day after day— blessings of joy, of health, of prosperity, of family, and of friends! I rejoice in the work you give me to do and in the quiet times in my day when I come to you and worship you. I rejoice when I'm tired, and I rejoice in you even when I am attacked by the devil. I delight in you even when my body is not feeling as I'd like. I rejoice at night. I rejoice during the day! God, you are really fabulous!

Rejoice in Righteousness

This righteousness is given through
faith in Jesus Christ to all who
believe. There is no difference between
Jew and Gentile.

ROMANS 3:22, NIV

Glory to God! I have the righteousness of God in
me because I have faith and personal trust in Jesus
Christ! I praise you, Father, that your righteousness is
available to everyone who believes in and confidently
relies on Jesus, because that means I'm conformed
to your Word and your promise! I'm rejoicing right
now that I am marching in accordance with your plan!
Thank you for filling me with your righteousness,
because I'm using that loving righteousness with my
family, my friends, and the people I work with every
day. Father, I love your righteousness!

Power of Faith

For I am convinced that neither death
nor life, neither angels nor demons,
neither the present nor the future, nor
any powers, neither height nor depth, nor
anything else in all creation, will be able to
separate us from the love of God that is in
Christ Jesus our Lord.

ROMANS 8:38-39, NIV

Father, my faith is rising to new heights! I thank you
that I am in your love and that nothing, absolutely
nothing, can separate me from your love! I'm
overwhelmed that your Word has made it so clear—
so powerfully plain and positive—that I can never
be moved from your love, which is in Christ Jesus
our Lord. I rejoice that your power guarantees me
your eternal love, no matter what the devil or any
of his demons try to pull, any time or any place. I'm
living in your divine love, regardless of any and all
circumstances!

Dead and Alive

I have been crucified with Christ; it is no longer I who live, but Christ lives in me; and the life which I now live in the flesh I live by faith in the Son of God, who loved me and gave Himself for me.

GALATIANS 2:20

Glory to God! I'm dead and alive at the same time! Thank you, precious Father, that I'm living a life that is really Jesus Christ living in me! I praise you, Father, because my worldly ways and sins were crucified on the cross with Jesus, who loved me and gave himself for me. The old me is dead—doubts, thoughts, habits, hurts, and memories—and I'm a completely new person, top to bottom, inside and out. Jesus rules the body I live in now, and I live in this body of flesh and bone by my faith in Him. Because of this, I'm a new person with nothing to hold me back! Father, I thank you that my new life glorifies you!

Encompassing Love

For God so loved the world that He gave
His only begotten Son, that whoever
believes in Him should not perish but have
everlasting life.

JOHN 3:16

Father, this is the day the world says is the day for lovers, but I don't have to depend on just this one day a year, because I'm living in your love every day of the year. Thank you that your love encompasses the entire world, and yet is personal just for me. Father, you said if I would simply believe in you, I would not perish, but have everlasting life. I believe, I believe, I believe! Thank you for the faith that lets me believe! I receive your gift of eternal life and I look forward to living forever with you.

Words of Faith

If anyone speaks, let him speak as the oracles of God. If anyone ministers, let him do it as with the ability which God supplies, that in all things God may be glorified through Jesus Christ, to whom belong the glory and the dominion forever and ever. Amen.

1 PETER 4:11

Father, I thank you that as I speak, I speak as a prophet of God, because my mouth shall speak your words. My words are pleasant words like a honeycomb, sweet to the soul and health to the bones. I praise you because I have a wholesome tongue, which is a tree of life. My mouth is also a well of life. I guard my tongue so that I am not snared with the words of my mouth. My heart retains your words, and out of the abundance of my heart, shall I speak! Amen!

He Cares for Us

Casting all your anxieties on him,
because he cares for you.

1 PETER 5:7

Here are my cares, Father! This means *all* of my
worries, anxieties, and concerns. I'm giving them all
to you once and for all! Your love overwhelms me! I
thank you for taking all of my worries and cares away
because you love me so much and you don't want me
to be burdened. My anxieties are gone! Just as in the
story of the prodigal son, you don't care what I've
done or where I've been; you love me and care for
me no matter what. Father, I'm so glad to be home at
last with you. I rejoice because I'm your child, forgiven
and restored by your mercy and loving kindness to my
inheritance in your kingdom. I praise you, Father, that
my ways have been changed because you care for me!
Hallelujah! I don't have any more worries I have cast
them upon you.

Heart of Flesh

I will give you a new heart and put a new
spirit within you; I will take the heart of
stone out of your flesh and give you a
heart of flesh.

EZEKIEL 36:26

Father, I'm so thankful that I have a new heart
and a new spirit within me! Thank you, Father, that
you've taken my stony heart out and replaced it with
a heart filled to the brim with love! I love you! I love
my friends! I love my family! I even love my enemies
because of what you have done for me! I never have
to worry about running out of love because you keep
filling me up with more, more, more! I thank you,
Father, that I can love you with all of this new heart
you've given me, and I thank you that with my new
spirit I now live righteously.

FEBRUARY 18

Follow His Light

> Then Jesus spoke to them again, saying, "I am the light of the world. He who follows Me shall not walk in darkness, but have the light of life."
>
> JOHN 8:12

It's fun walking in the light, Father, because Jesus is the light of the world! Thank you, Father, for the light you gave me through your Son, Jesus. By this wonderful, brilliant light I walked out of the gloom of darkness and left it behind forever! Now I can see the way because the path of new life in Jesus shines brightly. Darkness holds no more fear for me because it's gone from my life, and I am walking and leaping and praising God in the light! I glory in the light of Jesus, and I follow where He leads me. In His light, I am happy, I am healthy, and I am prosperous! In His light, I am fulfilled and victorious! His light *is* my life!

His Wisdom

If any of you lacks wisdom, let him ask
God, who gives generously to all without
reproach, and it will be given him.

JAMES 1:5, ESV

I praise you, Father, because I have wisdom! I have
all the wisdom I need to prevail over any challenge.
Your Word says if I don't have it, all I have to do is ask,
and you will give it to me, liberally and ungrudgingly.
Thank you for giving me the kind of wisdom that
triumphs over worldly knowledge every time, because
worldly knowledge doesn't compare to your wisdom.
You are a giving God, so I have all the wisdom I need
to live and work and make decisions righteously and
victoriously. I have wisdom in all my dealings with
others, and I praise and thank you for it!

Abundance of Blessings

Don't love money; be satisfied with what
you have. For God has said, "I will never
fail you. I will never abandon you." So we
can say with confidence, "The Lord is my
helper, so I will have no fear. What can
mere people do to me?"

HEBREWS 13:5-6, NLT

I am gloriously satisfied, Father, in the overflowing
abundance of divine blessings you have showered
upon my life! I am content in your love! I praise you
that there isn't any room left in me for greed or
for envy of what my neighbors have, because your
constant presence in my life is wealth far above the
material things of this world. I'm not afraid of what
anybody can do to me since you've assured me that
you are my helper, and no one can prevail over my all-
powerful God. Father, I don't have to rely on worldly
security, because you are everything I need! I praise
you because you never relax your hold on me. You
never let me go! Glory!

Move Your Mountain

For assuredly, I say to you, whoever says
to this mountain, "Be removed and be
cast into the sea," and does not doubt in
his heart, but believes that those things he
says will be done, he will have whatever
he says.

MARK 11:23

Jesus, I believe in you and your holy Word! Your
Word and your promises empower me to have what
I desire when I pray. My desires align with your
Word and what you want for me. Therefore, I say I
have wisdom! I have health! I have happiness! I have
prosperity! I have abundance! I have joy! I have love!
Father, I say to every mountain in my life, "Be removed
and be cast into the sea." Jesus, you give me strength
and perseverance to face every obstacle that arises.
No mountain will stand in the way of following you
and your will for my life.

Desires of the Heart

Therefore I say to you, whatever things you ask when you pray, believe that you receive them, and you will have them.

MARK 11:24

Father, I believe right now! I've prayed, and the minute the words came out of my mouth, I believed! I thank you, Father, that you didn't tell me to wait until I built up enough faith to believe, but to believe the very instant I prayed so that I could have the things that I desired. I praise you, Father, that because I take delight in you, you give me the desires of my heart, and that's why I know, that I know, that I *know* that you're going to fulfill the desires that you yourself have placed there! Glory, Father! Thank you for the faith you've given to me to see this come to pass.

FEBRUARY 23

Living Water

On the last and greatest day of the festival, Jesus stood and said in a loud voice, "Let anyone who is thirsty come to me and drink. Whoever believes in me, as Scripture has said, rivers of living water will flow from within them."

JOHN 7:37-38, NIV

Father, I'm thirsty, thirsty, thirsty! I'm drinking at your streams of living water deeper and deeper all the time. I thank you because that same river of living water I'm drinking now blesses me and blesses everyone around me as it flows from my innermost being. Father, I praise you for giving to me a river of living water that never runs dry, but keeps flowing and flowing. Thank you for that refilling station you've given me to use day and night. Thank you because it is open twenty-four hours a day. Father, I love you for that!

FEBRUARY 24

The Ultimate Rescuer

> Be sure of this: The wicked will not go
> unpunished, but those who are righteous
> will go free.
>
> PROVERBS 11:21, NIV

Father, how I praise you for such a promise. My faith is in you and not in what I see. I see much wickedness around me, but you are holy, just, and true. You see the works of the wicked and you will make all things right in due time. The wicked will be overthrown and the house of the righteous will stand. My house will stand because we are standing on the promises of your Word. You have set me free and I will enjoy eternal life because of your saving grace. Thank you!

FEBRUARY 25

Be Fruitful in Him

For this reason we also, since the day we heard it, do not cease to pray for you, and to ask that you may be filled with the knowledge of His will in all wisdom and spiritual understanding; that you may walk worthy of the Lord, fully pleasing Him, being fruitful in every good work and increasing in the knowledge of God.

COLOSSIANS 1:9-10

Father, I praise you that I am being filled with the knowledge of your will in all wisdom and spiritual understanding. I thank you that I am constantly learning your ways and purposes and that you are giving me discernment of spiritual things. I praise you because you have given me these blessings, I am walking worthy of you, Lord, and am fruitful in every good work, steadily growing and increasing in my knowledge of you. I thank you that all my decisions are ordered by you! Glory!

Filled to the Brim

I am coming to you now, but I say these
things while I am still in the world, so that
they may have the full measure of my
joy within them.

JOHN 17:13, NIV

Father, I thank you because I am filled with joy! The
joy of the Lord is my strength, so I'm strong because
my cup is filled to the top and overflowing with joy.
You have anointed me with the oil of gladness. I sing
and shout with joy because I have favor with God and
man, so I'm always a winner. My joy is contagious and
flows over to reach others, and today I'm speaking
love, joy, and peace to everyone I meet. Thank you for
telling me the things that have put joy in my heart! I'm
bubbling, bubbling, bubbling over because your full
measure of joy is within me.

Reborn

For you have been born again not of seed which is perishable but imperishable, that is, through the living and enduring word of God.

1 PETER 1:23, NASB

I'm born again of incorruptible seed! Father, I can't thank and praise you enough for lifting me out of the darkness and sin of the world, where mortal life leads only to death. Your Word makes me made new, regenerated, and reborn to eternal life in your kingdom. I am in this world of corruption and decay, but I am not of it because the perfect seed of your Word has made me into an entirely new person. Father, I praise you that your Word lives and abides forever! Because of this, I shall live forever, too!

A Child of God

The Spirit Himself bears witness with our spirit that we are children of God, and if children, then heirs—heirs of God and joint heirs with Christ, if indeed we suffer with Him, that we may also be glorified together.

ROMANS 8:16-17

Father, how I thank you for letting me clearly know that I can never be lost or alone because the Holy Spirit says that I am your child! I know where I belong. Thank you, Father, that I am a joint heir with Jesus. You gave everything you had to Him so I share fully in the entire inheritance. Father, I'm so rich because of your promises. Because I am a joint heir with Jesus, I am your temple and your Spirit dwells in me! I thank you that I have power to overcome all obstacles in this world. You are my God and I am your child. I claim your promise that all things in heaven and earth belong to me!

FEBRUARY 29

Real Life

Therefore I say to you, do not worry about your life, what you will eat or what you will drink; nor about your body, what you will put on. Is not life more than food and the body more than clothing?

MATTHEW 6:25

Thank you, Father, for another beautiful month where I had the opportunity to love you more than ever before and to study and grow in your Word. Father, your Word and your promises have become real in my life in ways that make me love you more and more. I thank you that your Word endures forever and that I have victory in you. I don't have to take thought for my life because my life is in you, Father, and you supply *everything*. I thank you that the kingdom of God is not meat and drink, but righteousness, peace, and joy in the Holy Ghost. I have health! I have abundance! I have joy! I have peace! I have Jesus!

MARCH

Abundance

Jesus came that we would have abundant life (see John 10:10). He wants us to be fruitful and bear *much* fruit—spiritually, physically, emotionally, and mentally ... at home, work, in our relationships, finances, health, and more.

And He told us how we can be fruitful: *"Abide in Me, and I in you. As the branch cannot bear fruit of itself, unless it abides in the vine, neither can you, unless you abide in Me. I am the vine, you are the branches. He who abides in Me, and I in him, bears much fruit; for without Me you can do nothing"* (John 15:4–5).

As you meditate on the following Scriptures and declarations this month, let them draw you into His presence to be near to His heart and abide with him. Glorify Jesus by bearing much fruit and living in His abundance, because Jesus said, *"By this My Father is glorified, that you bear much fruit; so you will be My disciples"* (John 15:8).

Divine Health

Beloved, I pray that you may prosper in all things and be in health, just as your soul prospers.

3 JOHN 2

Father, I rejoice in the desire you have for prosperity and health in my body and my soul! Thank you for being such a wonderful and loving Father who takes care of me in such full and overflowing measure. Thank you for the secret of prosperity, which lies in giving to you so that you can multiply it back to me. I'm not going to hold tight to what I have, Father, but instead, I'm keeping my hands empty and open so you can keep filling them up with more! And I'm placing the same trust in you for my health, knowing how generously you provide. Thank you for the blessing of wonderful and divine health that I live in all this year. Your Word is my life, so my soul is prospering!

My Whole Heart

"Bring the whole tithe into the storehouse, that there may be food in my house. Test me in this," says the LORD Almighty, "and see if I will not throw open the floodgates of heaven and pour out so much blessing that there will not be room enough to store it."

MALACHI 3:10, NIV

Here it is, Father, my whole tithe. I'm giving it to you! You are the best financial advisor I could possibly have! I'm giving generously into your storehouse, Almighty God, because it pleases you to "throw open the floodgates of heaven" and to let the blessings gush out in abundance upon me. I am made in your image, so I know you want me to be generous as you are generous in giving to me until I have no room for more! I receive the gift of your blessed abundance with thanks and praise, and I'm giving to you, Father, fully trusting in your promise of return. I'm expanding my mind and my ability to receive your blessings to make more room for that flood that is pouring out of those floodgates.

Sinners Storing for Me

To the person who pleases him, God gives
wisdom, knowledge and happiness, but to
the sinner he gives the task of gathering
and storing up wealth to hand it over to
the one who pleases God.

ECCLESIASTES 2:26, NIV

Father, those who do not follow you are working to
gather and store up wealth to give to the righteous
who are in right standing with you. Glory! Thank you
for giving me wisdom, knowledge, and happiness! I
rejoice because you teach me that covetousness and
greed are meaningless, for you take the wealth sinners
have gained and give it to those who please you,
for your way is righteousness. I receive that sinner's
money right now so I can have more to give to you. I'm
blessed by your marvelous generosity, Father.

Multiplied Harvest

Cast your bread upon the waters, for you
will find it after many days.

ECCLESIASTES 11:1

Heavenly Father, I love to cast my bread upon your
waters, and I praise you for the way you multiply it
and send back many times over what I give! Thanks
for showing me that the real secret of receiving is
to give with a loving heart, because when I put my
whole trust in you, everything always comes back
magnified. Father, I thank you that I am able to give
love, kindness, a helping hand, time, money, and gifts
whenever you tell me because it's your good pleasure
to replace it to me from your own unlimited store
house. I've cast my bread upon the water, Father, and
I thank you for the great harvest that is coming back
to me!

All Things

But seek first the kingdom of God and His righteousness, and all these things shall be added to you.

MATTHEW 6:33

Father, I praise and thank you for the truth of the promises in your Word! You said *all things* shall be added to me, and I believe every word of it! I am craving and earnestly seeking everything in the kingdom of God. You never fail me. You have gathered me into your kingdom and your righteousness, and here I am, jubilantly rejoicing because of it! You give me everything I need, not because of what I do or don't do, but because I'm a member of your very own family, loved and cared for, from now through eternity. I hold out my hands to you, Father, and claim your promise that *all* things are added to me. I have love, joy, peace of mind, health, and abundance. I have *all* things! Father, you're so good to me that I can't glorify you enough!

Sun and Shield

For the LORD God is a sun and shield;
the LORD bestows favor and honor; no
good thing does he withhold from those
whose walk is blameless.

PSALM 84:11, NIV

Father, you are my sun and shield! I love you for promising that you will not withhold one single good thing from me. I rejoice to walk uprightly in your light because in your light, I can always know how to handle any situation. Your shield protects me from the devil's barbs, his lies, his deceits, and I rejoice that he runs away from your light! Protected by your shield and illumined by your light, my life is blessed by an abundance of your gifts, for you are a God of grace and glory! I glorify your name, Father, because you supply all my needs and more! Thank you for the heavenly bliss and favor you generously bestow on me. I confidently commit all I am and all I have to you!

Abundant Giving

Give, and you will receive. Your gift will return to you in full—pressed down, shaken together to make room for more, running over, and poured into your lap. The amount you give will determine the amount you get back.

LUKE 6:38, NLT

Father, how I bless you for your money-back guarantee, which guarantees that when I give to you, it shall be given back to me. When I give love, you give me an exceeding abundance of love. When I give time, you return that time to me over and over again. When I give money, you give it back to me in full and plenteous amounts. I praise you that you use what I give as a measuring spoon to dish out what you give to me, so I don't ever need to be limited by anything except what I am willing to give. Father, I'm giving my all and everything I am and have to you, and I thank you that I am walking in a super abundant supply!

Seeds of Giving

Remember this: Whoever sows sparingly
will also reap sparingly, and whoever sows
generously will also reap generously.

2 CORINTHIANS 9:6

How I praise you, Father, for the wonderful harvest
you are bringing forth in my garden! Thank you for
teaching me how to be a successful farmer. Thank
you for teaching me to sow generously and joyfully in
great abundance so you can bless it and return it to
me multiplied beyond my wildest dreams! Thank you
for the harvest you have prepared for me. Thank you
for teaching me not to be stingy in any area of my life,
whether it is in love, health, joy, or finances. I plant
in faith, generously, and you open the floodgates of
heaven to pour blessings on me! I thank and praise
you, Father, for the exploding abundance of all things
you bring about from the seeds of my giving!

Store Your Treasure

Do not lay up for yourselves treasures on earth, where moth and rust destroy and where thieves break in and steal; but lay up for yourselves treasures in heaven, where neither moth nor rust destroys and where thieves do not break in and steal. For where your treasure is, there your heart will be also.

MATTHEW 6:19-21

I'm not storing my treasures up here on the earth, but I'm storing them up in heaven with you, Father, where I don't have to worry about moths and rust, or even thieves who break through and steal. Father, I'm banking my treasure with you because you are the most reliable trust company in the entire world. You are a living river of blessings, and I praise you for taking care of your children with loving interest! My treasure is in heaven with you, and my heart is right up there too!

MARCH 10

Riches in Glory

And my God shall supply all your need according to His riches in glory by Christ Jesus.

PHILIPPIANS 4:19

My needs are gloriously and liberally supplied! Thank you, Father, for sending Jesus to die on the cross as a ransom for my sins because through Him I have abundant new life! I praise you not only for paying all my bills, but also for taking care of me in countless invisible ways: providing love when I need it, lifting my spirit, sending a friend when I need a helping hand, directing your angels to guard my family. Over and over, you surprise me with your miraculous timing in providing answers to even unspoken prayers of mine! Father, I rejoice that my needs are fulfilled—faithfully and constantly—by your wonderful and inexhaustible riches found in glory by Christ Jesus!

Supply and Demand

> The bin of flour was not used up, nor did
> the jar of oil run dry, according to the
> word of the LORD which He spoke by
> Elijah.
>
> 1 KINGS 17:16

My jar of oil shall never fail, because I shall never eat my seed! I praise you, Father, that when the widow was willing to listen to your prophet and share what she had instead of eating it all with her son, you kept filling the barrel of meal and pouring oil into the jar. Father, how we bless you for giving us instructions on how to have our needs met at all times. I praise you that even though the supply looks low at times, I can rest assured that you're always there to put in what I need!

MARCH 12

Inheriting the Kingdom

I love those who love me; and those who
diligently seek me will find me. Riches and
honor are with me, enduring wealth and
righteousness. My fruit is better than gold,
even pure gold, and my yield better than
choicest silver. I walk in the way of
righteousness, in the midst of the paths of
justice, to endow those who love me with
wealth, that I may fill their treasuries.

PROVERBS 8:17-21, NASB

Father, how I love your Word and all the promises
you have for me. I thank you that enduring wealth and
uprightness in every area of my life is mine! I thank
you that you even allow me to inherit substance, often
from sources I never knew about, and that you fill my
treasuries. I am indeed wealthy because my riches are
heavenly and divine. Thank you that you have taken
charge of my earthly bank account and fill it with
divine deposits! Glory!

House of Blessing

The curse of the LORD is on the house of
the wicked, but He blesses the habitation
of the just.

PROVERBS 3:33

Father, my house is blessed! I rejoice that you are a
God of justice. No thought or act escapes your notice,
and you know which are the houses of the wicked
and which are the houses of the righteous. You see
through all the deceptions of the wicked; there is
no way they can hide from your curse. But I praise
you because you also see directly into the hearts and
minds of the righteous, and you never forget to bless
and reward your children who serve you faithfully.
Look into my heart and my mind, dear Father, because
I rejoice in praising you! I glory in your wonderful
blessings!

Endless Love

The blessing of the LORD makes one rich,
and He adds no sorrow with it.

PROVERBS 10:22

I praise you, Father, for filling my life with the treasure of your blessing, which makes me rejoice day after day. I am rich in you! I am rich in your endless love, which feeds me like manna from heaven! You put food on my table, clothes on my back, and smiles on my face and the faces of my family! Glory, Father! How can I thank you enough? You give me health, happiness, and prosperity! You guard me from temptation and teach me with the wisdom of your Word! You renew and refresh my spirit so I can face each day with joy! Father, I praise you for not adding sorrow to my life, because with all your blessings, there just isn't room for it!

The Giver and Receiver

And so I tell you, keep on asking, and you will receive what you ask for. Keep on seeking, and you will find. Keep on knocking, and the door will be opened to you. For everyone who asks, receives. Everyone who seeks, finds. And to everyone who knocks, the door will be opened.

LUKE 11:9-10, NLT

Glory! Hallelujah! Hallelujah, Father! I'm an asker, a seeker, and a knocker, and because of this, I'm a receiver. Thank you that your Word says if I ask it shall be given to me! Thank you that you didn't say *some* will receive but you said *everyone*, including me! When I ask, *you* give to me; when I knock, *you* open the door; when I seek, *you* guide me safely to my destination. I'm asking, Father, and therefore, I have what I ask for. I have love! I have joy! I have health! I have prosperity! Thank you for being such a loving and generous Father to me!

For the Table

He provides food for those who fear him;
he remembers his covenant forever.

PSALM 111:5, ESV

Oh, glorious Father, you are the river of life, the provider of all my well-being! I rejoice every day because you remember me without fail. You not only put the food on my table, but you nourish my soul and protect me from all physical harm. Because I am your child, you love me. I eat the food you give me with a hearty appetite, delighting in each bite because I know who has provided it and who will always provide it. Father, I am thankful for everything you give me, for it all belongs to you. I am blessed by your caring, sharing, loving, and wonderful faithfulness to me! Hallelujah! I praise you that your covenant is forever imprinted on your mind so that you will remember it throughout all of eternity.

MARCH 17

Whole Works

The LORD is my shepherd; I shall not want.

PSALM 23:1

You are my shepherd and I shall not want. I shall not want for health! I shall not want for finances! Father, your promises are magnificent, *big* promises! Your love for me is so great that you want me to have every good thing! I thank you and praise you, heavenly Father, because you say plainly and clearly that I shall not want! You are my God, and I am your child! You are my shepherd, and I follow where you lead! I rejoice because you are the kind of Father who wants me to personally prosper in this life and share your eternal glory in the next! Father, I'm blessed beyond words! I shall not want for joy! I shall not want for happiness!

MARCH 18
· · · · · · · · · · · ·

Loaded

Blessed be the Lord,
Who daily loads us with benefits,
The God of our salvation!

PSALM 68:19

I'm loaded, but not with problems! Father, I thank you for loading me with the good things of life every day! I don't have to live on yesterday's blessings or wait for tomorrow's blessings because you send fresh blessings each day. I'm singing and shouting my praises up to you because you give me a taste of heaven right on this earth! You are the God of my salvation and all glory belongs to you. Every moment of this day is special to me because you are always right here with me, and you know what benefits I need much better than I do! I love you, praise you, and bless your name, Father, for all I'm receiving today. Thank you that I don't have to have only monthly or weekly blessings, but that you supply them on a daily basis! Hallelujah!

Good Gifts

Yes, the LORD will give what is good, and
our land will yield its increase.

PSALM 85:12, ESV

I can't help praising you, Father, because you know
how to give good gifts. You have given me life and you
have removed the curse of sin from my life through
the sacrifice of your only begotten Son on the cross.
I thank you for my new life and my salvation. I thank
you for Jesus Christ. I thank you for the Holy Spirit.
Yes, Father, you give what is good and my heart
rejoices. My arms are open wide to receive your gifts! I
love you with all my heart, all my soul, all my mind, and
all my strength. Because of your goodness, Father, my
land is blessed with a rich harvest and I am prosperous.

Your Voice Alone

And all these blessings shall come upon
you and overtake you, because you obey
the voice of the LORD your God.

DEUTERONOMY 28:2

I'm ready, Father, to be overcome and overtaken
with blessings! I will not listen to the devil; I'm listening
to your voice only. I've cleaned out my ears, and I'm
hearing even the tiniest little word you say to me.
I'm singing your praises and rejoicing because you've
promised that your blessing will catch up with me
and simply overwhelm me. I want to peek over my
shoulder and watch them arrive, Father, because I've
inherited even the blessings you gave to Abraham.
Because Jesus took my sins away, I am restored to
your favor. I praise you for the abiding love you have
for your people, which has flowed down through the
centuries to reach me. I bless you because I live under
your blessings. I heard the condition to your blessings
too, Father, so I'm doing my part and following your
instructions completely!

City and Field

Blessed shall you be in the city, and
blessed shall you be in the country.

DEUTERONOMY 28:3

Heavenly Father, you will bless me wherever I am—
in the city or the country. I rejoice that your blessing
follows me wherever I go! I thank you that you are my
shield and protection from evil in the city! I thank you
that you are my strength and my rest in the field! You
are with me wherever I go, so that my way is blessed
and prosperous. My work goes well and my life bears
fruit that pleases you. Because you love and bless me, I
am not swallowed up in the confusion and darkness of
the world. I rejoice, Father, because you are with me!

Bread of Life

Blessed shall be your basket
and your kneading bowl.

DEUTERONOMY 28:5

   How I rejoice, Father, that I don't have to worry about inflation, the price of food, and shopping. I praise you that complex economic policies, the rise and fall of the stock market, and business red tape don't have any effect on your blessings. Heavenly Father, when you say my basket is blessed, *it is blessed*! My kneading bowl, or my bread, is blessed because I'm feasting on Jesus—the bread of life! Your blessings come as promises in power and in truth! You are my God. Nations rise and decay under your hand, but your blessings remain with me through thick and thin! Father, I will not worry because I'm too busy praising and thanking you to have time for it!

In and Out

Blessed shall you be when you come in,
and blessed shall you be when you go out.

DEUTERONOMY 28:6

I'm blessed coming in, and I'm blessed going out!
Father, when I knock on the door, you open it so I
can come in and I am blessed! When I go out to seek,
you help me to find what I'm seeking, and again, I'm
blessed! Father, only through you I am I assured of
getting blessed whether I'm coming or going! I praise
you, heavenly Father, for directing my way, because
in your glorious wisdom, I am guided to the door of
opportunities that bless me. I am guided out the door
to better opportunities that bless me again. I rejoice
and thank you, Father, that you care for me enough to
always bless my coming in and going out.

MARCH 24

All Conditions

The LORD will cause your enemies who rise against you to be defeated before your face; they shall come out against you one way and flee before you seven ways.

DEUTERONOMY 28:7

Enemies, get ready to go! I thank you, Father, that those who come against me with evil in their hearts will never find me alone, but I am always safe with you. I praise you because in your righteousness and power, you defeat my enemies and strike confusion into their ranks so they run before me in seven different ways! Father, even when I am under attack, I'm still blessed because I stand firm and glorify you before the world for causing the defeat of unrighteousness. Thank you, heavenly Father, for blessing me under all conditions! I can't lose with you, Father, because I'm blessed when they attack me, and I'm blessed when they leave me alone!

The Storehouse

The LORD will command the blessing on you in your storehouses and in all to which you set your hand, and He will bless you in the land which the LORD your God is giving you.

DEUTERONOMY 28:8

Everything I undertake is blessed— what a promise! Father, I praise you because when you command something to be done, *it is done!* Thank you for commanding a blessing upon me personally, for the projects I've already started and the things I'm going to do in the future. Father, I work with your praises upon my lips because you bless and reward those who are faithful to you. I don't worry about my savings, because your blessing protects what is mine better than any bank vault. I'm not anxious about the success of anything I tackle because under your blessing, my work prospers! Father, you have blessed me in everything you have given me, and I am grateful to you. Hallelujah!

MARCH 26

Surplus Goods

And the LORD will grant you plenty of
goods, in the fruit of your body, in the
increase of your livestock, and in the
produce of your ground, in the land of
which the LORD swore to your fathers to
give you.

DEUTERONOMY 28:11

Thank you, Father, that your Word promises more
than bare sufficiency; your Word promises *plenteous
goods!* I rejoice and praise you because your plan for
me is a life of abundance, not just scraping by day-to-
day. I thank you because everything I do multiplies and
bears fruit in the power of your generous and loving
blessing upon me and upon my land. Father, you are
a fountain of blessings to me and I glorify your name!
I have more than enough, and I will always have an
excess, an oversupply, and a balance left over to give
to others in need! Hallelujah!

MARCH 27

The Good Treasury

The LORD will open to you His good treasure.

DEUTERONOMY 28:12

Father, when I think that you open to me your good treasure, I know it means everything you've got is open and available to me. I feel like a child, full of excitement, sticking my hand in a grab bag of goodies! Some things in a grab bag are disappointing, but Father, *all* of the things in your treasury are good! I rejoice because it is truly your pleasure to give me the kingdom. When you open something up, you don't open just a little crack, but you open it wide. I thank you and rejoice that you are the one who's doing it, Father, and that you don't make me try to chisel my way inside of something difficult to get into. You open it up to me—free of charge. How I love you for your generosity!

Righteous Hands

A good man leaves an inheritance to his children's children, but the wealth of the sinner is stored up for the righteous.

PROVERBS 13:22

I glorify you, Father, because you are providing for me a rich inheritance to leave my children and my children's children. My family line will be blessed for every generation until you return because you are blessing me today and guiding me in your paths of righteousness. Heavenly Father, I thank you that I am also leaving an inheritance of moral values and good behavior to my children and my children's children, both through the example I set for them and through teaching them your Word. Father, I lift my hands up right now to be a funnel for you to pour the sinner's wealth into me, and I receive your abundance. Amen!

Precious Plans

Commit your works to the LORD, and your
thoughts will be established.

PROVERBS 16:3

My plans are established and succeeding! What a
promise! I praise you, Father, because when I bring my
intentions, plans, and ideas to you before I start on
any project, you conform my thoughts and will so that
everything I do succeeds wonderfully. Even if I come
to you with wrong ideas, you roll them all upon you,
committing them to your precious care. You turn my
thoughts around so that I think in the right direction.
I'm letting all of my thoughts go straight to you.
Without you, my thoughts could go off track and get
me into trouble; but with you, my plans are established
and succeeding. Hallelujah!

No Weapon

"No weapon formed against you shall prosper, and every tongue which rises against you in judgment You shall condemn. This is the heritage of the servants of the LORD, and their righteousness is from Me," says the LORD.

ISAIAH 54:17

Father, I rejoice that my heritage in you protects me from the weapons of enemies and the tongues of the wicked or mistaken people who speak against me. My righteousness is in you, so I have nothing to fear. The devil and his deceptions are turned away from me and are brought to nothing by your power because my faith is in you, and you are my shield and my buckler. Thank you for wrapping your shield of faith around me so that I can confidently face the world and know that no weapon of any kind that is formed against me can prosper in any way because of your Word!

Words of Power

So shall My word be that goes forth from My mouth; It shall not return to Me void, but it shall accomplish what I please, and it shall prosper in the thing for which I sent it.

ISAIAH 55:11

   Glory, Father, that your Word goes forth with power and it does what you intend it to do! I thank you because your promises and your blessings prosper me and my works, exactly as you want them to. I thank you for your loving kindness, for the many blessings you have poured out upon me this month, and for your constant presence in my life. I praise you because you are a God of power, glory, and righteousness, and because the Word that goes forth from your mouth with such wonderful authority brings me joy, peace, love, happiness, friendship, health, and prosperity as I let those same words flow through my mouth!

APRIL

The Name of Jesus

Confess the following prayer every day this month, along with the one for each day, to firmly establish in your mind that He is risen:

"Thank you, Father, that we can say Jesus is risen. When they went to the tomb, He was not there! It was empty! Jesus, thank you for dying on the cross and taking all of the sins of mankind upon yourself. You established forever that your name is above all other names when you arose victoriously out of the bonds of hell and over the power of Satan. Thank you, Father, for the resurrection power that made salvation possible."

Each day as you make your declaration, whether you are alone or with someone, say it out loud, and say it with authority until the declaration that is written becomes your declaration! The name of Jesus is above every other name!

A Beautiful Name

Therefore God has highly exalted him and
bestowed on him the name that is above
every name, so that at the name of Jesus
every knee should bow, in heaven and
on earth and under the earth, and every
tongue confess that Jesus Christ is Lord,
to the glory of God the Father.

PHILIPPIANS 2:9-11, ESV

Jesus, Jesus, Jesus. How I love that name! I thank
you, Father, for giving your Son such a beautiful name.
Thank you for your power in that name. I praise you
that the name of Jesus is over and above sickness,
disease, poverty, demons, and everything else the
devil tries to give me. I take the name of Jesus over
any plague that tries to come near my dwelling,
because that name is above all things inside and out.
My tongue confesses daily that Jesus Christ is Lord.
Jesus is Lord! *Jesus is Lord!*

On My Lips

Then He arose and rebuked the wind, and said to the sea, "Peace, be still!" And the wind ceased and there was a great calm.

MARK 4:39

Father, how we praise you! We know that if we call upon the name of Jesus, the wildest storm that is blowing around us will be still and quiet. When the enemy comes, the name of Jesus muzzles whatever the devil is trying to do. My heart shall have peace all day today because whenever the wind starts to blow, I shall take the name of Jesus on my lips. Thank you for the peace that passes all understanding that rests in my heart because of what you've given to us in the name of Jesus!

Name Above All

That the name of our Lord Jesus Christ
may be glorified in you, and you in Him,
according to the grace of our God and the
Lord Jesus Christ.

2 THESSALONIANS 1:12

Father, it has been over 2,000 years since you sent your Son to walk on this earth. I can't stop talking about His miraculous life and I can't thank you and praise you enough for sending Him. I thank and praise you for giving me the opportunity to have Jesus glorified in me by the way I live my life before others, and to be glorified, myself, because I live in Him. Thank you, Father, because this can only happen by your grace and that of our Lord Jesus Christ. Thank you for that beautiful name above all names, the name of Jesus! I take it upon my lips daily in thanksgiving for what you have done for me.

His Healing Power

And the whole multitude sought to touch Him, for power went out from Him and healed them all.

LUKE 6:19

He healed them all! What a statement, and what a truth! I praise you and exalt the name of Jesus because Jesus and His name are one, Father! There was so much power in His very being, His presence, that the ever-present virtue flowed out of Him and healed every person. I thank you because you have given me the same power and the authority to use the name of Jesus to let healing virtue flow out of me. I praise you that Jesus was victorious in all circumstances and at all times, therefore, because I am a joint heir with Him, I am victorious and triumphant at all times because of that name: *Jesus!* Name above all names!

Ask and Receive

"In that day you will ask nothing of me. Truly, truly, I say to you, whatever you ask of the Father in my name, he will give it to you. Until now you have asked nothing in my name. Ask, and you will receive, that your joy may be full."

JOHN 16:23-24, ESV

Your goodness is overwhelming. My joy is full and running all over the place! I thank you, Father, that Jesus said *whatever* I ask in His *name*, you will give to me. I rejoice and give thanks that the name Jesus has such power and authority. I'm blessed to ask in the name of Jesus because of the love that fills my heart when His name is on my lips and because of the sweet expectation of receiving what I ask from you. Thank you for giving so bountiful in my life that my joy is running over!

Remain in Christ

You did not choose Me, but I chose you
and appointed you that you should go
and bear fruit, and that your fruit should
remain, that whatever you ask the Father
in My name He may give you.

JOHN 15:16

You chose me! You ordained me! You picked me
out because you wanted to! I thank you, Father, that I
am chosen and ordained through Jesus Christ to bear
fruit in my life from the love and truth He expresses
in me. Thank you that I live so that people can see the
love of Jesus in me and that I can reach out to tell the
Good News to others. Thank you that I am appointed
to bring forth fruit and that my fruit will remain as
your Word says, so that I can ask for anything in Jesus'
name and you will give it to me! So I ask that my life
will bear much fruit, and that fruit will remain.

Greater Works

Very truly I tell you, whoever believes in me will do the works I have been doing, and they will do even greater things than these, because I am going to the Father. And I will do whatever you ask in my name, so that the Father may be glorified in the Son. You may ask me for anything in my name, and I will do it.

JOHN 14:12-14, NIV

I believe in you, Jesus. I get so excited when I read that I can do even greater things than you did. My mind can't comprehend all the things you've promised, but I believe them because you have said so in your Word. I thank you that your Word makes such a complete and total statement. When you picked the word *whatsoever*, I know that if I asked in the name of Jesus, it will be done! Father, I want to glorify your Son in all that I do! I'm walking in power because you said so!

APRIL 8

Holy Gifts

Peter said to them, "Repent, and each
of you be baptized in the name of Jesus
Christ for the forgiveness of your sins; and
you will receive the gift of the Holy Spirit."

ACTS 2:38, NASB

Father, I rejoice and thank you for the power that's
in the name of Jesus! I thank you that at with your
name, the lame shall walk, the blind shall see, and
healings shall take place today just as they did in the
days when the disciples walked on this earth. I thank
you for the blessings that the name of Jesus brings. I
thank you for the gift of the Holy Spirit. Thank you for
the power that comes with the Holy Spirit. Thank you
for the joy that comes with the Holy Spirit. I praise you,
Father, that you give *all* of your blessings to *all* of your
children. I'm not going to miss a single one!

Sign Posts

And these signs will follow those who believe: In My name they will cast out demons; they will speak with new tongues.

MARK 16:17

Glorious Father, how I praise and thank you that in the name of Jesus I have power over devils. They all know who Jesus is, and I don't have to fear them one bit because the devil himself trembles at the very name of Jesus! Thank you, Father, that all the powers of darkness are afraid and run away at the mention of Jesus, because through Him, they and every evil plan are defeated. What a blessing you give to us, Jesus, when we speak with new tongues. Thank you, Father, for the language of love you give us with which to praise you and love you. Thank you that this is for all believers, and that includes me! Thank you for these signs!

Hands of Healing

They will be able to handle snakes
with safety, and if they drink anything
poisonous, it won't hurt them. They will be
able to place their hands on the sick, and
they will be healed.

MARK 16:18

Thank you, Father, that as I look at my hands I don't see anything powerful. I don't see anything unusual; I don't see much of anything except fingers on each hand. But your Word says that in the name of Jesus, these ordinary hands can be laid on sick people and *they will recover!* I praise you for not saying maybe, or that only some would be used, but you just simply said that the hands of believers would be used! I'm a believer, Father, and even though I might not be able to feel power flowing through my hands at all times, by faith in your Word, I know it's there, and I know that the sick will recover when my hands are laid upon them! Thank you that my family is made whole by the use of my hands!

Bold Declaration

So they called them and commanded
them not to speak at all nor teach in the
name of Jesus. ... Saying, "Did we not
strictly command you not to teach in this
name? And look, you have filled Jerusalem
with your doctrine, and intend to bring
this Man's blood on us!" But Peter and
the other apostles answered and said:
"We ought to obey God rather than men."

ACTS 4:18, 5:28-29

   Thank you, Father, that the name of Jesus has so
much power that the devil and his cohorts flee at the
very mention of His name. People were so afraid at the
mention of the name of Jesus they forbade Peter and
John to ever speak of His name. Thank you for their
boldness in saying, "We ought to obey God rather than
men." I praise you that I can use that same boldness
today, say the exact same words, and be a God-pleaser
and not a people-pleaser. Thank you for the power in
Jesus' name.

Coming into the World

And those who went before and those who followed were shouting, "Hosanna! Blessed is he who comes in the name of the Lord!"

MARK 11:9, ESV

Father, I thank you that I come in the name of the Lord, because I am a child of God, redeemed by the blood of the Lamb, the sacrifice of Jesus Christ on the cross, and because of the word of my testimony. I rejoice and praise you, Father, that because I come in His name, I am blessed. Thank you for sending your Son, Jesus, to prepare the way for us to follow Him. I'm singing and shouting His praises because I come in His name!

Heavenly Home

Heaven and earth will pass away, but My
words will by no means pass away.

MATTHEW 24:35

Father, it is beyond my comprehension that this
earth will some day pass away, and that the sun,
moon, and stars that I've seen and been used to all
my life will pass away. But I believe it because your
Word says so! I rejoice that the things of your eternal
kingdom shall not pass away, and that you have
chosen me to spend eternity in your glorious kingdom
because of my salvation in Jesus Christ! How I thank
you for sending your Son, and praise you for your
Word in which I will stand on all the days of my life. It
lifts my spirit up to the heavenly places when I think of
these wonderful promises!

All Authority

Behold, I give you the authority to trample
on serpents and scorpions, and over all
the power of the enemy, and nothing shall
by any means hurt you.

LUKE 10:19

That is real power, Father! I thank you because
Jesus unreservedly gave me the power to walk on
things that would seek to harm me. I thank you that
this power was magnified to give me power over all
the enemy, without possibility of retaliation upon me,
because Jesus guaranteed that nothing would be able
by any means to hurt me. I praise you, Father, because
Jesus didn't limit my power to particular conditions,
and didn't say I only have power over part of the
enemy, but over *all* the enemy's power! Thank you,
Father, that nothing is going to hurt me because Jesus
gave me that power in His name!

Show the Way

Assuredly, I say to you, whoever does not receive the kingdom of God as a little child will by no means enter it.

LUKE 18:17

Glory, Father! I'm so thankful because getting into your kingdom is so simple that I'm going to shout out your praises! What a blessing that I am not required to have a college degree. I don't even have to speak Greek or Hebrew, and I don't have to belong to a certain club or be an expert in anything. I'm so glad that you let me join your special club just by simple faith in the blood of Jesus. I didn't gain access by intellect, meditation, or muscles. There wasn't anything to figure out. I didn't have to buy a ticket and there was no red tape. How I praise you, Father, that you sent Jesus to show me the way! I humbly and gratefully receive your wonderful gift.

Impossible Made Possible

But He said, "The things which are impossible with men are possible with God."

LUKE 18:27

I will not be limited by what others say can or cannot be done. I praise you, Father, because there is an infinitely greater hope, an infinitely greater power than what man or science says I can do. Because Jesus said it, it became so! Those very things, which are impossible with men, are possible with you. Thank you, Father, that through you I can expect the impossible and the miraculous to happen! You are the changeless God! You are the same God of miracles today as you were 2,000 years ago, or in Moses' time, or at creation! I am glad that you are *my* Father!

Lost Became Found

For the Son of Man has come to seek and
to save that which was lost.

LUKE 19:10

He searched for me. He hunted me. He pursued
me. He sought me! Thank you, Father, for sending
your very own Son, Jesus, to rescue me when I was
lost in the darkness of sin. I thank you that you loved
me so much, you let your own Son bear my sins upon
the cross, so that I might be cleansed and saved from
eternal damnation. I was lost, but He found me and
saved me so I could become part of your kingdom!
I rejoice that Jesus shined His light on the path that
led me right to your gate! Father, I will praise you and
glorify your name forever that your Son was sacrifice
so I could have eternal life! I thank you that you are
seeking to save all that which is lost—every person,
every thing—and that everyone I know and love will
come to know you and enter your kingdom. Thank
you, Father!

Good Tidings

Do not sorrow, for the joy of the Lord is
your strength.

NEHEMIAH 8:10

Jesus gives joy! Glory to God! I sing hosanna to the
highest because of the joy that overflows in my heart.
I praise you that the redeemed of the Lord shall return
and come with singing unto Zion, and everlasting joy
shall be upon their heads. How I praise you that they
shall obtain gladness and joy, and sorrow and sighing
shall flee away. I can rejoice because my name is
written in heaven. Father, I thank you for the beautiful
words of the angel when he said, "Behold, I bring you
good tidings of great joy!" (Luke 2:10). Thank you that
the Good News was Jesus and the good tidings still
bring joy today. Father, I'm walking and leaping and
praising you because of the overabundance of joy in
my heart! And that joy is my strength.

Without Bondage

Therefore if the Son makes you free, you shall be free indeed.

JOHN 8:36

Most assuredly, I say to you, if anyone keeps My word he shall never see death.

JOHN 8:51

I'm free, I'm free, I'm free indeed. I am liberated. I am unconditionally set free! I am unquestionably set free because Jesus set me free. Father, I thank you for the freedom I have in this beautiful country of mine, but I thank you much more for the freedom Jesus came to bring me! Thank you that you sent Jesus to free me from bondage to sin and to free me from death, which your Word says is the wages of sin. I rejoice and praise your name, Father, because now I shall never see spiritual death! I have a glorious eternal life ahead of me, and I'm enjoying it this very minute! Thank you, Father! Hallelujah!

The Evil One

The thief comes only to steal and kill and
destroy. I came that they may have life
and have it abundantly.

JOHN 10:10, ESV

The devil is good for nothing! He steals, he robs, he
plunders, he hijacks, he swindles, he blackmails, he
cheats, and he tries to destroy everything that comes
his way! Father, how I love you that Jesus came to give
me the abundant life by restoring me to your love,
the source of all abundance! I thank you that the devil
who comes as a thief, is powerless to steal the new
life I have in you because he has to run from the very
name of Jesus! Thank you, Father, for my new life of
abundance—love, joy, health, abundance, and eternal
life in your kingdom! Hallelujah!

A Precious Kernel

Most assuredly, I say to you, unless a grain
of wheat falls into the ground and dies, it
remains alone; but if it dies, it produces
much grain.

JOHN 12:24

I see a whole wheat field, Father, swaying in the
breeze of the Holy Spirit. How I thank you that Jesus
died on the cross and rose again the third day, to bring
forth the fruit of salvation in me so I could have eternal
life in your kingdom! I thank you that I'm part of that
fruit crop! If that one kernel had not died, Father,
there would have never been a way for me to have
eternal life. My sins were washed away in the blood of
the Lamb you sent as a living sacrifice for me! I rejoice
because I'm a new person living a new life in your love,
and all of this was made possible through one precious
kernel—your lovely Son Jesus!

Washed and Wed

And such were some of you. But you were
washed, but you were sanctified, but you
were justified in the name of the Lord
Jesus and by the Spirit of our God.

1 CORINTHIANS 6:11

Father, I praise you that I have been washed
absolutely clean and spotless and purified by the blood
of Jesus, which has provided complete atonement
for my sin. I have been set free from the guilt of sin,
and I am set apart, consecrated, purified, sanctioned,
and authorized in that name that is above all names! I
praise you that I have been pronounced righteous, and
all the things that you held against me before I was
saved are now just as if they had never happened. I
take that wonderful name upon my lips at all times and
tell the world about the wonderful things that happen
in that name!

APRIL 23

Divine Peace

Peace I leave with you, My peace I give
to you; not as the world gives do I give
to you. Let not your heart be troubled,
neither let it be afraid.

JOHN 14:27

Your peace certainly is different from the world,
Father! I rejoice and thank you for that very special
kind of peace that Jesus gives to me. I praise you that I
don't have to be agitated and disturbed by happenings
in the world because that's not the kind of peace you
give. That special peace is a divine peace that calms
my heart and mind in exactly the same manner Jesus
did when He commanded a storm to cease when
His disciples in the boat became afraid. I praise you,
Father, that nothing and no one can ever trouble my
heart or take away the peace that Jesus gave me,
because it's divine, and it's mine!

Abiding Love

If you abide in Me, and My words abide in you, you will ask what you desire, and it shall be done for you.

JOHN 15:7

Jesus, I'm abiding in you! I'm vitally united to you through your Word, and I'm letting your words settle down deep inside of me, into all the dark corners of my life so that they will permanently dwell, reside, live, and stay within me at all times. I'm speaking your words. I'm living your words. I'm loving your words! I'm blessed and thankful to be always with you and your abiding love, to be able to ask *anything* of you and know that it will be done. Father, I praise you and bless you because you are always there to provide answers to my problems, to love me and nourish me and lift me up! I'm soaring higher all the time because I'm abiding in you and you're abiding in me!

Hope of Glory

To them God has chosen to make known among the Gentiles the glorious riches of this mystery, which is Christ in you, the hope of glory.

COLOSSIANS 1:27

Thank you, Father, that you have made known to me what was once a mystery to the Gentiles—that Jesus Christ lives right inside me! I praise you because with Jesus, I have the riches of glory, the power to live righteously in this world, and the hope of eternal life in your kingdom! Thank you, Father, that it pleases you to make this mystery known to me, so I can live by faith in your grace through Jesus Christ, and let my light shine before mankind! I don't know how He does it, Father, and that's not important! The important thing is that He does!

Characteristics of God

And have put on the new self, which is being renewed in knowledge in the image of its Creator. ... Therefore, as God's chosen people, holy and dearly loved, clothe yourselves with compassion, kindness, humility, gentleness and patience.

COLOSSIANS 3:10,12, NIV

I'm sparkling. I'm clean. I'm shiny, and I'm new! Father, thank you that I am a new person in Christ, with a new spiritual self that is continually renewed and perfected in knowledge, after the image of my Creator. Thank you that I'm being sanctified and made holy as one of your elect. To do your works I've been given your characteristics—mercy, kindness, humility, meekness, patience, and willingness to endure whatever comes before me. Thank you, Father, for your love, because these things would never be mine in the flesh, but they are mine because of you.

Your Holy Work

For God did not call us to uncleanness,
but in holiness.

1 THESSALONIANS 4:7

I praise you, Father, for your Word, which speaks loud and clear. My calling is not just a part-time job where I can do your holy work part of the time and fool around with sin at other times. Thank you that you want me all of me all the time! I praise you that I don't have unclean desires and thoughts because you protect and shield me from the filth that the devil throws at me. Thank you, Father, as I follow Jesus Christ and abide in Him, that the power of righteousness now flows through me and I am victorious in Christ!

Divine Wisdom

If any of you lacks wisdom, let him ask of God, who gives to all liberally and without reproach, and it will be given to him. But let him ask in faith, with no doubting, for he who doubts is like a wave of the sea driven and tossed by the wind.

JAMES 1:5-6

Father, I thank you for all the things I can ask in the name of Jesus. Thank you for telling me that if I lack wisdom, all I have to do is ask and it is mine, given liberally without question. I rejoice in the strength of faith I have to ask and receive from you, and I thank you that I'm not blown this and that way like a weather vane. Thank you, Father, that my faith is steady and constant. I really appreciate that even though I might be very deficient in natural wisdom, because I have asked, I have received divine wisdom because I have the mind of Christ!

Submit to God

Submit yourselves therefore to God. Resist the devil, and he will flee from you. Draw near to God, and he will draw near to you. Cleanse your hands, you sinners, and purify your hearts, you double-minded.

JAMES 4:7-8, ESV

Devil, I'm resisting you, and you will flee from me! Thank you, Father, that I can come before you with clean hands and a pure heart. I submit myself completely to you, giving thanks because as I draw near to you, you come closer and closer to me. I praise you, Father, that I have power not only to resist the devil, but to chase him away completely. He has to flee before your power. No longer will I be double-minded with wavering and divided interests, but I shall be single-minded, desiring only to serve and love you! The devil can't touch me!

Kingdom Come

> For if you remain completely silent at this
> time, relief and deliverance will arise for
> the Jews from another place, but you and
> your father's house will perish. Yet who
> knows whether you have come to the
> kingdom for such a time as this?
>
> ESTHER 4:14

Father, you sent your Son to this world at just the
right time, and you brought me into this world for such
a time as this. Thank you that your timing is perfect
in all things. I am excited about that day when your
perfect timing will close the world as I know it today.
In the midst of the world's failing systems, thank you
that I stand on that solid rock of Jesus! You will bring
relief and deliverance to others through my life. I am
available, Father, and I glory in your perfect timing!

MAY

Blessings

God loves us so much that His heart cries when we don't avail ourselves of all the blessings He wants to give us. Look how easy He makes it for us:

Christ has redeemed us from the curse of the law, having become a curse for us (for it is written, "Cursed is everyone who hangs on a tree"), that the blessing of Abraham might come upon the Gentiles in Christ Jesus, that we might receive the promise of the Spirit through faith ... And if you are Christ's, then you are Abraham's seed, and heirs according to the promise (Galatians 3:13–14, 29).

Every blessing that belonged to Abraham belongs to you and to me. Hallelujah!

MAY 1

Meditate On Your Words

Blessed is the man who walks not in the counsel of the ungodly, nor stands in the path of sinners, nor sits in the seat of the scornful; but his delight is in the law of the LORD, and in His law he meditates day and night. He shall be like a tree planted by the rivers of water, that brings forth its fruit in its season, whose leaf also shall not wither; and whatever he does shall prosper.

PSALM 1:1-3

Father, I'm blessed, blessed, blessed! I'm happy, fortunate, and prosperous because I don't follow the advice, plans, or purposes of the ungodly. Just lead them to me and I'll share the Good News. I certainly am not going to sit down with the scoffers and mockers, but I constantly meditate in your laws and your words. Your promises are music to my ears and sweet as honey in my mouth. I thank you that everything I do in you prospers in a marvelous way because my joy is in your law.

The Shepherd

The LORD is my shepherd; I shall not want. He makes me to lie down in green pastures; He leads me beside the still waters. He restores my soul; He leads me in the paths of righteousness for His name's sake.

PSALM 23:1-3

I lack nothing in my life, Father, because you lead me to beautiful places where I am nourished and at peace, both physically and spiritually. Father, I praise you and thank you for that, because you are my shepherd, my light, and my hope. You feed and clothe me and restore my soul when I'm weary because you love me as a shepherd loves his flock. I thank you that whenever I'm rushing around too much, you lead me beside the still waters, out of the turmoil of life. Thank you, Father, for protecting me from the wolves of the world and for leading me in the paths of righteousness.

Walking Through

Yea, though I walk through the valley of
the shadow of death, I will fear no evil; For
You are with me; Your rod and Your staff,
they comfort me. You prepare a table
before me in the presence of my enemies;
You anoint my head with oil; My cup runs
over.

PSALM 23:4-5

Father, thank you that I don't walk into the valley
of the shadow of death and sit down. No, you've
said that I walk *through* the deep, sunless valley of
the shadow of death. Hallelujah, I'm walking right
out of that valley whether it be sickness, poverty, or
depression, and I fear no evil because you protect me.
Thank you for preparing a spiritual feast for me right in
front of my enemies!

Fill the Cup

You anoint my head with oil; My cup runs over. Surely goodness and mercy shall follow me all the days of my life; and I will dwell in the house of the LORD Forever.

PSALM 23:5-6

How I rejoice, Father, that I'm so blessed, because you anoint my head with so much of the oil of the Holy Spirit that my cup runs over. You don't give me just a little trickle; you give me a cup that runs and runs and runs over! Thank you, Father, because two things are going to follow me all the days of my life: goodness and mercy! Not sorrow and sadness, but goodness and mercy, and I thank you because I'm blessed to be able to dwell in the house of the Lord forever!

Precious Blood

Blessed is he whose transgression is
forgiven, whose sin is covered.

PSALM 32:1

I'm blessed! I'm happy! I'm fortunate! I'm to be
envied! All because my sins are forgiven! My sins are
covered by your precious blood in such a way that
you can't even see them. I'm walking on air because
a huge burden has been lifted from my shoulders and
replaced by that wonderful blessing because *all* my
sins are gone. How I thank you that the blood of Jesus
was sufficient to cover the sins of the whole world,
including mine, and I praise you that when you forgive
sins you also forget them. I'm a brand new person
to you. Thank you for the tremendous and unending
supply of love you've poured out on me!

Desires of Your Heart

Delight yourself also in the Lord, and He shall give you the desires of your heart. Commit your way to the Lord, trust also in Him, and He shall bring it to pass.

PSALM 37:4-5

I delighted in you and with you, Lord, and my heart is overflowing with good measure. You see deep and directly into my heart, and you give me the desires of my heart because you have taken out the carnal desires of the flesh I once had, and you have replaced them with your divine desires. You even grant those secret requests that no one knows about except you and me. Since I've committed my life to you and trust you completely, you give me what I desire, the best things, not substitutes or imitations. No one has a better father than I do, because you are my Father, and your promises stagger my wildest imagination. Hallelujah! I'm blessed because you're bringing good things to pass! Glory!

His Mercy Endures Forever

Oh, give thanks to the Lord, for He is good!
   For His mercy endures forever.
Oh, give thanks to the God of gods!
   For His mercy endures forever.
Oh, give thanks to the Lord of lords!
   For His mercy endures forever.

*Read the rest of Psalm 136 and
then make the following declaration:*

Heavenly Father, I'm blessed because you are a good God and your mercy endures forever. I've committed sins that seem to be unforgivable, but in your mercy you have forgiven them. You've given me a beautiful world in which to live because of your mercy. Because of your mercy, you have given me friends who delight my heart and you've kept my enemies off my back. Lord, you didn't have to do any of these things for me, but you did, because of your mercy. Thank you, Father, that your loving kindness and mercy—which are not temporary but eternal, everlasting blessings—will continue unceasingly and eternally! They never wear out, or go sour, but last forever and forever!

You Never Depart

You have hedged me behind and before,
and laid Your hand upon me. Such
knowledge is too wonderful for me; it is
high, I cannot attain it. Where can I go
from your Spirit? Or where can I flee from
Your presence? If I ascend into heaven,
You are there; if I make my bed in hell,
behold, You are there. If I take the wings
of the morning, and dwell in the uttermost
parts of the sea, even there Your hand
shall lead me, and Your right hand shall
hold me.

PSALM 139:5-10

Father, I'm blessed by your glorious presence
wherever I go, whether I'm in Arkansas, New York,
Zambia, or China. If I were an astronaut, Father, I'd
find you in outer space. I rejoice in the blessing of
your presence from which I never want to depart, for
it's your hand that guides me along the straight and
narrow path. Thank you, Lord, for your presence in my
life. Thank you that I can never be lost to your sight!

My Rock

Blessed be the LORD, my rock, who
trains my hands for war, and my fingers
for battle; he is my steadfast love and
my fortress, my stronghold and my
deliverer, my shield and he in whom I take
refuge, who subdues people under me.

PSALM 144:1-2, ESV

Father, I'm blessed because your keen strength
and supreme power protect me under all conditions
no matter how difficult they look. I'm blessed,
too, because your strength makes me a spiritual
warrior armed with the razor-sharp sword of your
righteousness, so that I actively take part in the war
against darkness. I'm blessed because you never leave
me nor forsake me and your steadfast love surrounds
me at all times. You are my high tower of safety, my
deliverer, and my shield to protect me from the darts
of the devil at all times, and you subdue those enemies
who try to attack me! I glory in such a glorious God!

Spiritual Blessings

Blessed be the God and Father of our Lord
Jesus Christ, who has blessed us with
every spiritual blessing in the heavenly
places in Christ.

EPHESIANS 1:3

All spiritual blessings in heavenly places are mine!
I give you praise and adoration because you are the
Father of our Lord Jesus Christ, the Messiah. I rejoice
that Jesus is with you in heaven and is preparing a
place for me there. I'm ready for that wonderful day
when He will come to take me home to you. In the
meantime, I'm going to enjoy all the Holy-Spirit-given
blessings in heaven and earth that you've passed on to
us through your wonderful Son! Glory!

The Blessings of Abraham

But Christ has rescued us from the curse
pronounced by the law. When he was
hung on the cross, he took upon himself
the curse for our wrongdoing. For it
is written in the Scriptures, "Cursed is
everyone who is hung on a tree." Through
Christ Jesus, God has blessed the Gentiles
with the same blessing he promised to
Abraham, so that we who are believers
might receive the promised Holy Spirit
through faith. … And now that you belong
to Christ, you are the true children of
Abraham. You are his heirs, and God's
promise to Abraham belongs to you.

GALATIANS 3:13-14, 29

I'm redeemed by the blood of the Lamb! I've been
redeemed from the curse of the law because of Jesus
Christ. Thank you for sending my Lord Jesus to wash
my sins away and remove the curse that separates
me from you and your love. Your love lifts and blesses
me constantly. Thank you, Father, for your endless
blessings and for making me an heir to all the promises
of Abraham. I am a part of your family!

Reaping a Harvest

Do not be deceived: God cannot
be mocked. A man reaps what he
sows. Whoever sows to please their
flesh, from the flesh will reap destruction;
whoever sows to please the Spirit, from
the Spirit will reap eternal life.

GALATIANS 6:7-8

I'm overcome with blessings today, Father, because you've promised that whatever we sow, we shall reap. I'm sowing a bumper crop of love, joy, and peace today, Father. I'm not planting my seed in the infertile soil of the flesh because I don't want to reap corruption; I'm sowing to the spirit to be able to reap life everlasting! I praise you that my life is not down here, but my real life is in heaven with you and Jesus! I'm blessed because you make this all possible for me personally, and how I love you for that!

Through Faith

And raised us up together, and made us sit together in the heavenly places in Christ Jesus, that in the ages to come He might show the exceeding riches of His grace in His kindness toward us in Christ Jesus. For by grace you have been saved through faith, and that not of yourselves; it is the gift of God, not of works, lest anyone should boast.

EPHESIANS 2:6-9

Glory to God, you've raised me up, and I'm sitting in heavenly places in Christ Jesus. I love you for that. Thank you, Father, that my salvation is not dependent upon my good works, but is entirely dependent upon the exceeding riches of your grace. You so simply said if I would believe in Jesus Christ, His work at Calvary, His blood, and confess it with my mouth, I would be saved. Hallelujah, Father, I'm saved and filled with your love! I can't boast about it, either, because you did it all!

Dwells in You

That Christ may dwell in your hearts through faith; that you, being rooted and grounded in love, may be able to comprehend with all the saints what is the width and length and depth and height— to know the love of Christ which passes knowledge; that you may be filled with all the fullness of God.

EPHESIANS 3:17-19

Thank you, Father, for blessing me with the knowledge that Christ lives in my heart because I trust in Him. I am rooted and firmly grounded in that tremendous love, which is so long, so wide, so high, and so deep that I will never really be able to understand the greatness of this love for me. Thank you, Father, for the knowledge that some beautiful day I will be filled all the way up to the top with you! What a promise! I don't deserve it, but I receive it!

The Full Armor

Finally, be strong in the Lord and in his mighty power. Put on the full armor of God, so that you can take your stand against the devil's schemes.

EPHESIANS 6:10-11, NIV

I praise you, Father, for blessing me with your strength, and the power of your might! Because you provided my whole armor, it is invincible, unconquerable, unyielding, and indomitable! I am blessed because even though I don't wrestle against flesh and blood, but against principalities, against powers, against the rulers of the darkness of this world, and against spiritual wickedness in high places, you have given me your whole armor to wear for protection. With the power of your might going before me, Father, I will always be victorious!

Promises Kept

Praise the LORD who has given rest to his people Israel, just as he promised. Not one word has failed of all the wonderful promises he gave through his servant Moses.

1 KINGS 8:56

What a blessing it is to serve you, Father. When the world lies, cheats, and fails to keep its word, you are always right there, fulfilling all of your promises. Thank you that the God of Abraham, Isaac, and Jacob knows my name too! Thank you for being a God of integrity, Father, so that I can be an imitator of you and be a person of integrity in all of my dealings. Thank you that all of the blessings of Abraham are mine because your Word promises this; you never fail to keep your promises. Hallelujah, what a God I serve! I'm blessed!

Be Fruitful

Then God blessed them and said, "Be
fruitful and multiply. Fill the earth and
govern it. Reign over the fish in the sea,
the birds in the sky, and all the animals
that scurry along the ground."

GENESIS 1:28, NLT

Father, I'm being overtaken and overcome with
blessing, again, because of your love. I'm blessed. I'm
blessed because I have dominion over the fish of the
sea, over the fowl of the air, and all living things! I'm
blessed because I can be used to multiply your family.
I'm blessed because I am fruitful. I'm blessed because
I was made in your likeness. I'm blessed because this
blessing is upon both man and woman alike, in whom
there is no difference in your sight. Glory!

Given to You

Arise, walk in the land through its length
and its width, for I give it to you.

GENESIS 13:17

Father, what blessings you give me. Thank you for
the privilege of knowing that all the blessings you
bestowed in the beginning of creation have flowed
down, through time, to me. Thank you for letting me
walk through the length and breadth of the land you
have for me, knowing that you will give it to me. Thank
you for blessing those who bless me and who bring
happiness upon me. Thank you that I can be a blessing
also to others by dispensing good to them. Thank you
for giving me so much land and possessions that I can
share generously with others! How I bless you for all
your blessings! I'm walking forward, backward, and
sideways over the land you give to me!

MAY 19

The Same

Jesus Christ is the same yesterday,
today, and forever.

HEBREWS 13:8

Father, I praise and thank you that your Son alone, among all the constant changes taking place in the world, always remains the same. I thank you that because of this, He still saves, heals, and delivers. You are the living cornerstone of my life, and I am saved, healed, and delivered because He hasn't changed one single bit and never will! I thank you that when the price of gold soars to new highs or drops to new lows that Jesus is exactly the same. Thank you for blessing me with a changeless Savior, my healer, my doorway into your marvelous glorious presence. He is my rock, and I can rely on His sameness forever.

Patiently Perfecting

Therefore be patient, brethren, until the coming of the Lord. See how the farmer waits for the precious fruit of the earth, waiting patiently for it until it receives the early and latter rain.

JAMES 5:7

Heavenly Father, thank you for the blessed hope I have in the coming of my Lord Jesus Christ. I'm blessed now, Father, because He lives in my heart, waiting for exactly the chosen day to come to me in person. Thank you for your Word, Father, which tells me that Christ is like the farmer who waits for the seasonal rains to bring His crop to ripeness before the harvest time. I praise you, Father, for patiently perfecting me in your love so I'll be joyously prepared for that great day! Hallelujah!

Endures Forever

For you have been born again, not of
perishable seed, but of imperishable,
through the living and enduring word of
God. For, "All people are like grass, and all
their glory is like the flowers of the field;
the grass withers and the flowers fall, but
the word of the Lord endures forever."
And this is the word that was preached to
you.

1 PETER 1:23-25

Father, I'm born again and I'm filled with your joy.
The incorruptible seed of your Word has been planted
in my heart and is growing every day! I praise you,
Father, that although the things of this world come
and go, your Word, a priceless eternal treasure,
endures forever. Thank you for the blessing of your
living, enduring Word! You are not temporary; you are
eternal, everlasting, and never wear out!

MAY 22

Eternal Life

For God so loved the world that He gave
His only begotten Son, that whoever
believes in Him should not perish but have
everlasting life.

JOHN 3:16

Thank you, Father, that because of your love I can
answer my phone and say, "God loves you!" and
feel your love going right through that phone to the
person on the other end. Thank you, Father, that
you love us so much, your imperishable blessings are
available to us. Thank you that I am blessed because
you loved me enough to send your only begotten
Son, Jesus, to die for me so that I might have eternal
life! I love you, Father! I believe and am grateful for
everlasting life.

A Royal Priesthood

But you are a chosen generation, a royal priesthood, a holy nation, His own special people, that you may proclaim the praises of Him who called you out of darkness into His marvelous light.

1 PETER 2:9

I'm glad I'm different and unique! I'm blessed to belong to a chosen race, a royal priesthood, a holy nation, a member of your own purchased, special people. I can set forth and show to all the world your wonderful deeds and display the virtues and perfections of your divine nature. You have gifted me to minister to the spiritual needs of those around me. My Lord is King of kings and Lord of lords, who has the power to call whosoever He will out of the darkness and death into the marvelous light of new life. Thank you, Father, for giving me the blessing of Jesus and your love in Him. I'm peculiar and I want the world to know the reason for it! Hallelujah!

Open to Your Prayers

For the eyes of the Lord are on the righteous, and his ears are open to their prayer. But the face of the Lord is against those who do evil.

1 PETER 3:12

Hallelujah, I can't hide from you, Father. I'm so blessed that your eyes are upon the righteous, those who are in right standing with you. Your Word says that you are attentive and sensitive to my prayers. I'm blessed because your ears are open to me twenty-four hours a day. How I praise you for never tiring of listening to me. Thank you that I am never lost to your sight, but under your tender, loving care at all times. How I praise you that you differentiate between the evil and the righteous because I would never want to have you turn your face from me! I'm never going to even try to hide from you!

Pleasing to God

And whatever we ask we receive from
Him, because we keep His commandments
and do those things that are pleasing in
His sight.

1 JOHN 3:22

Whatever I ask is mine because I keep your
commands and am pleasing in your sight! What a
promise, Father! I'm blessed because you've given me
instructions for life that are written down in a book
that I can refer to constantly. You shower me with so
much love that I rejoice to obey everything you tell me
to do! You bless me with your faithfulness, so I bless
you with mine! I watchfully and carefully obey all your
instructions and do the things that are pleasing in
your sight. I observe your suggestions and constantly
practice what is pleasing to you. I thank you for being
willing to do whatever I ask because my wishes are
in line with what you want for me! I'm swimming in
blessings!

Overcoming Fear

There is no fear in love: but perfect love
casts out fear, because fear involves
torment. But he who fears has not been
made perfect in love.

1 JOHN 4:18

Father, I'm blessed that I have no fear in me
whatsoever because I'm protected by your power
and strength from all the things of the devil. By your
Word, I have no fear in me and dread does not exist.
Your full-blown, perfect love turns fear away from
me and gets rid of every trace of terror. I'm blessed,
Father, and I praise you that I'm not suffering the
torment of darkness because you've lifted me into the
wonderful light and complete perfection of your love.
Thank you, Father, for blessing me! Regardless of the
circumstances, your love overcomes all fear!

Angels Watching

Are they not all ministering spirits sent forth to minister for those who will inherit salvation?

HEBREWS 1:14

Thank you, Father, for sending out your angels who are ministering for us constantly because we are heirs of salvation. Thank you, Father, for blessing us with the knowledge that those same angels are bringing our loved ones to that person who will minister salvation to them. Thank you that you send angels forth even without me knowing about it. Thank you for letting them minister for my protection in times of trouble. They keep my foot from slipping when the path gets dangerous. Thank you that your angels can even close the mouths of lions so that they are not a danger to a child of God. I'm blessed because of angels!

Eyes of Your Heart

I keep asking that the God of our Lord
Jesus Christ, the glorious Father, may give
you the Spirit of wisdom and revelation,
so that you may know him better. I
pray that the eyes of your heart may be
enlightened in order that you may know
the hope to which he has called you, the
riches of his glorious inheritance in his holy
people.

EPHESIANS 1:17-18, NIV

Glory, Father, for your blessings are overwhelming
me with joy. You have granted me a spirit of wisdom,
revelation, and insight into mysteries and secrets in
the deep and intimate knowledge of your Son. You
have flooded the eyes of my heart with light, giving me
the privilege of understanding what is the hope of my
calling and the riches that are the glorious inheritance
of your set-apart ones! I'm blessed because of the
magnitude of your blessings!

God's Generosity

For you know the grace of our Lord Jesus Christ, that though He was rich, yet for your sakes He became poor, that you through His poverty might become rich.

2 CORINTHIANS 8:9

Father, your blessings stagger my imagination! I am overwhelmed when I consider that Jesus had everything in your kingdom with all its riches and glories for Himself, yet, He chose to become poor for my sake that I could become rich in you. I praise you that I have been delivered from the curse through Him. I bless you that I am saved through grace because there is no way I could have earned the gift Jesus gave me. It was His kindness and His gracious generosity that make this all possible. I thank you that because of His poverty, I have become enriched and abundantly supplied at all times! I thank you that I am progressively becoming acquainted with these blessings more and more all the time!

Fix Your Eyes

So we fix our eyes not on what is seen, but on what is unseen, since what is seen is temporary, but what is unseen is eternal.

2 CORINTHIANS 4:18, NIV

Thank you, Father, for giving me spiritual eyes so that I don't have to look and see things the way the world sees them. I can look at them through your eyes. Thank you that I don't have to see only the things which are visible to our human eyes, but I can see with my spiritual eyes the glorious things of your kingdom, which is my inheritance. I praise you for this great blessing! I bless you because even though I've never seen you, I *know* you're there at all times, loving and protecting me.

Fullness of God

Beware lest anyone cheat you through philosophy and empty deceit, according to the tradition of men, according to the basic principles of the world, and not according to Christ. For in Him dwells all the fullness of the Godhead bodily.

COLOSSIANS 2:8-9

Father, what an overwhelming thought to know that I am in Christ and He is in me. All the treasures of divine wisdom and all the riches of spiritual knowledge and enlightenment are stored up and are hidden in Him, and they are mine. I have everything because I am joined with Jesus Christ in salvation. Father, the world can't talk me out of what your Word says is mine! My joy and my faith are at an all-time high because they stand on what Christ has said. I don't look to the world for their shallow answers and intellectualism. I look to the Holy Spirit for my answers to life. Bless you, Father, that you tell me with no qualms that Jesus is the highest ruler! Not only that, He is mine! Hallelujah, therefore I have everything I need in Christ Jesus!

JUNE

Love

Love is our declaration for the month, and what an appropriate subject for the month of June when people think of love and marriage. The love of God for humans, and humans for God, is the most beautiful love in all the world. It is this love that makes us lovable to the world and makes it possible for us to love them. God loves to hear you tell Him how much you love Him, so say it every day, will you?

On June 11, we have asked you to pick out someone to love in a special way. Write and tell us what happened to you and to them (www.joanhunter.org), because of this special day of giving love!

If you want to see some problems disappear in a hurry, write all the problems you have on a piece of paper, and at the bottom write: "*Yet in all these things we are more than conquerors through Him who loved us*" (Romans 8:37). Confess it every day until you discover that every single one of those problems is conquered!

Overflowing Joy

As the Father loved Me, I also have
loved you; abide in My love. If you keep
My commandments, you will abide in
My love, just as I have kept My Father's
commandments and abide in His love.
These things I have spoken to you, that
My joy may remain in you, and that your
joy may be full.

JOHN 15:9-11

My joy is running over and spilling all over the place!
Thank you, Father, that in the same way you loved
Jesus, He has also loved me. Thank you, Jesus, that
because I keep your commandments, I abide in your
love all the time. I can abide in your love twenty-four
hours a day because your source never runs out and
is always available to me. Thank you that my joy is full
and running over. Thank you that you gave your joy
not as a temporary thing, but as a permanent, full-time
gift. Your joy, happiness, and excitement remains in
me and is full, complete, and overflowing at all times.

Overflowing Love

Jesus answered and said to him, "If anyone loves Me, he will keep My word; and My Father will love him, and We will come to him and make Our home with him."

JOHN 14:23

Jesus, I love you, I love you, I love you! Father, thank you that your Son is so lovable. Thank you that I can love Him at all times and keep His words because His words are true and right and holy! Thank you, Jesus, for giving me words that last forever and never change. How I praise you because you have come to live in me and make your home in me! Because your love overflows in me, I can love others—not just neighbors, but even enemies! I love you for being so close to me at all times! I thank you that your house is my house and my house is your house!

The Heart of Man

> But as it is written: "Eye has not seen, nor ear heard, nor have entered into the heart of man the things which God has prepared for those who love Him."
>
> 1 CORINTHIANS 2:9

I'm excited today because I can hardly wait to hear what you're telling me! I praise you, Father, that regardless of whether or not I have 20/20 vision, my eyes have not seen, nor are they capable of seeing all the love that you have for me. Thank you that regardless of how good my hearing is my ears will never be able to hear all the wonderful truths you have ready for me. My heart belongs to you, Father, and I'm rejoicing right now because I know you'll have something beautiful beyond words to put in it! Thank you that all these wonderful gifts are especially for me because you love me!

No Matter What

> But God demonstrates His own love toward us, in that while we were still sinners, Christ died for us.
>
> ROMANS 5:8

I was the worst of them all, and, yet, you still loved me! Thank you, Father, that you loved me in spite of what I was! You didn't look at my faults and failures, but you looked at what you wanted to see in me! How I praise you, Father, that you let your Son die because your love for me was so great that you were willing to let His blood be shed to save me. I receive your love and enjoy it every day because I remember what that love was willing to do! It thrills me when I realize that I didn't have to clean myself up in order for Jesus to be willing to die for me; He was willing to do it when I was a miserable character!

JUNE 5

Only Glory

However, the LORD your God would not
listen to Balaam but turned the curse into
a blessing for you, because the LORD your
God loves you.

DEUTERONOMY 23:5, NIV

Father, how I praise you that you wouldn't allow
Balaam to curse Israel because you loved your people
so much. You were willing to turn any curse into a
blessing each time Balaam opened his mouth. Thank
you, Father, that the love which reached your people
in the Old Testament times still reaches me today. I
love you for that, Father. I thank you that when my
mouth gets out of line and begins to say the wrong
things that don't glorify you, you can still turn my
words around to be a blessing to others! You turn
every curse into a blessing in Jesus' name.

Truly Blessed

Whoever has my commandments
and keeps them, he it is who loves me.
And he who loves me will be loved by my
Father, and I will love him and manifest
myself to him.

JOHN 14:21, ESV

I praise you, Father, that Jesus has given us commandments to keep, which make the Christian life so simple and straightforward to live. All we have to do is what you tell us to do and refrain from doing the things you tell us not to do. We are blessed and living in your love right now. How we praise you, Jesus, that you have promised to manifest yourself to us because we love you. You've said that you will let yourself be clearly seen and make yourself real to me at all times. I really love you!

He Is Love

He who does not love does not know God,
for God is love.

1 JOHN 4:8

Father, thank you that your Word tells me the greatest commandment is to love you with every fiber of my being, and the second is to love my neighbor as myself. I obey these commandments so that you will live in my heart and fill me up with even more love! I praise you because when you created me, you made me able to receive and to give love, for you are love, and the river of your love flows continually to your people! I rejoice in your love, Father, and I thank you for letting us know, in no uncertain terms, that there is plenty of love for all those who open their hearts to receive it! I love you, Father!

A Soft Heart

Dear friends, since God so loved us,
we also ought to love one another.

1 JOHN 4:11, NIV

Thank you, Father, for showing us that you love us so much that there isn't any excuse for us not loving one another! Thank you for giving me a soft heart and the ability to love all my brothers and sisters on this earth. I know I could never do this on my own, but because you love me through all my sin, all my faults, and all my failures, you give me the ability to love even those people who seem unlovable! Thank you, Father, for your Word teaches that everybody deserves love!

A Thankful Heart

We know how much God loves us, and we
have put our trust in his love. God is love,
and all who live in love live in God, and
God lives in them.

1 JOHN 4:16, NLT

I glorify your name, Father, because I know and
believe how much you love me. You washed my sin
away with the blood of Jesus and there just isn't any
way I can imagine a greater love than that. There isn't
any way I can thank you enough for what you did. But,
Father, I want to try by loving you with everything
I've got and by obeying you in all things. I thank you,
Father, that I dwell in love because of your love for me.
Because of the power of your love, I live in you and
you live in me.

Greater Love

This is My commandment, that you love one another as I have loved you. Greater love has no one than this, than to lay down one's life for his friends.

JOHN 15:12-13

Love is the greatest force in the world, Lord Jesus, and is the most powerful word in the Bible. I thank you for commanding me to love others in the same way that you loved me. Thank you that you not only gave your life for your friends, but you gave it for me, an enemy for many years. How I praise you for showing me the way to love others! I will express your love in me to those I meet, even to those who are hard to love.

God's Special Love

"And you shall love the LORD your God
with all your heart, with all your soul, with
all your mind, and with all your strength."
This is the first commandment.

MARK 12:30

Father, I love you with all my mind, my heart,
my strength, and my soul! Because you love me so
much, it's easy to love you in return. I worship you,
Father, because your first commandment concerns
love, which is what everyone in the world needs and
deserves. Thank you that in loving you, I receive the
power to love everyone. I will find a specific individual
to love today. I will concentrate on finding a person
who needs love, someone who does not have many
friends, and whose heart is crying out for love. I'm
going to love that person today with your special love.

Limitless Love

A new command I give you: Love one
another. As I have loved you, so you must
love one another.

JOHN 13:34, NIV

Thank you, Father, that Jesus gave me a new
commandment. I praise you that people know I am
His disciple because I love in a new way. I love others
as Jesus loved me! Thank you that Jesus loved me
enough to teach me, heal me, and save me from
sin by even dying for me! Thank you that this is
your limitless love flowing through me right now, a
powerful love that enables me to love everyone even
as Jesus did. Thank you, Father, that when I obey this
commandment to love others, I am at the same time
loving you with all my heart, my soul, my mind, and my
strength.

Filled with God's Love

Then Christ will make his home in your hearts as you trust in him. Your roots will grow down into God's love and keep you strong. And may you have the power to understand, as all God's people should, how wide, how long, how high, and how deep his love is. May you experience the love of Christ, though it is too great to understand fully. Then you will be made complete with all the fullness of life and power that comes from God.

EPHESIANS 3:17-19, NLT

Father, I praise you that Jesus lives in me! Jesus, be more and more at home in my heart! Thank you that my roots are going all the way down deep into your soil, which enables me to feel the tremendous depth of your love for me, even though I know I will never be able to comprehend it with my limited mind. Father, I'm so excited because you promise that some day I will be filled all the way up to the top with you! Glory!

JUNE 14

God's Glory

And the glory which You gave Me I have given them, that they may be one just as We are one: I in them, and You in Me; that they may be made perfect in one, and that the world may know that You have sent Me, and have loved them as You have loved Me.

JOHN 17:22-23

Father, I love you, I love you, I love you for so many different reasons, but especially for the glorious perfect unity I have in Christ Jesus. He lives in me and you live in Him; we're all perfected into one glorious body. Father, how you could ever love me as much as you love Jesus is beyond my human comprehension, but I praise you that you do love me just as much as you do Jesus!

Sacrificial Love

But Ruth said, "Do not urge me to leave you or to return from following you. For where you go I will go, and where you lodge I will lodge. Your people shall be my people, and your God my God. Where you die I will die, and there will I be buried. May the LORD do so to me and more also if anything but death parts me from you."

RUTH 1:16-17, ESV

Thank you, Father, that this verse can also apply to marriage. Thank you for giving my marriage and every married couple the most beautiful words to say to each other that can be said. How I thank you, Father, for encouraging me to stay together in marriage. Thank you for the sacredness of human love, as well as divine love, and for allowing me to love my spouse in greater ways because of your love pouring through me.

Have No Fear

There is no fear in love; but perfect love casts out fear, because fear involves torment. But he who fears has not been made perfect in love.

1 JOHN 4:18

Thank you, Father, that your perfect, complete, full-grown, faultless love turns away every trace of fear. I glory in the knowledge that the devil can't touch me with fear because your love is so complete and surrounds me like a glove. It safely wraps me in a love cocoon. I praise you, Father, for letting me grow into love's complete perfection because of your great love for me. Thank you for a love, which is without a blemish and unparalleled in human understanding, but which is mine because I belong to you. I love you, Father!

More Than Family

He who loves father or mother more than
Me is not worthy of Me. And he who loves
son or daughter more than Me is not
worthy of Me.

MATTHEW 10:37

Father, I love you more than anything in the
whole wide world! I praise you, Father, because you
command and demand that I love you more than a
mother or father or even my children. Thank you for
always knowing what is best for me. By giving you the
first place in my life to love you most, you've given
me the opportunity to love my own family even more
because of your love flowing through me. Thank you
for giving me the desire and the ability to love you
more than anyone and to cling steadfastly to you and
walk in your ways. Thank you, Father, because the
love of my family is based on you and not on my own
desires. You have first place in my heart!

Walk in Love

And walk in love, as Christ also has loved
us and given Himself for us, an offering
and a sacrifice to God for a sweet-smelling
aroma.

EPHESIANS 5:2

Father, I'm walking in love! I'm running in love! I'm
leaping in love, and I'm falling in love with Jesus! Thank
you for loving me so much and giving me someone so
lovable. I'm walking down streets with love, letting
it bless people who don't even like me. I'm talking in
love to everyone I meet, including those who try to
cheat me! I'm thinking in love, even when my thoughts
might be trying to go in other directions. I'm a lover
because you've put love into my heart!

Loved Much

Therefore, I tell you, her many sins have been forgiven—as her great love has shown. But whoever has been forgiven little loves little.

LUKE 7:47, NIV

Father, although I was the worst of the sinners, you forgave me so much. It's easy for me to love you wholeheartedly without any reservations whatsoever. I love you, Father, because you didn't just forgive a little, but you forgave everything you might have ever held against me. I love you so very, very much! As a result of your forgiveness, I walk in peace and in freedom from all the problems that are the result of sin! No wonder I love you so much!

JUNE 20

Team Up

Do not be unequally yoked with unbelievers. For what partnership has righteousness with lawlessness? Or what fellowship has light with darkness?

2 CORINTHIANS 6:14, ESV

Lord, I love you because you tell me exactly how to find favor in your eyes. Thank you for telling me that I'm not to team up with people who don't love you. My inner being tells me that I don't have anything in common with them. Darkness and light don't go together; neither do God and sin. Thank you, Lord, that I walk in the light! Thank you for saving me from mismatched alliances in marriage, in business, and in friendship. There's no way a partnership can work with you on one side and the devil on the other. Thank you for pointing it out to me so vividly to keep me from falling into dangerous places again!

Just as God

Instead, be kind to each other,
tenderhearted, forgiving one another, just
as God through Christ has forgiven you.

EPHESIANS 4:32, NLT

Father, thank you for giving me the power to forgive those who have sinned against me, and I praise you for telling me to be kind, tenderhearted, compassionate, and understanding because I belong to Christ. I love you, Jesus, for living in and through me, which gives me the power and the desire to forgive each and every person who may have ever hurt me. Father, I praise you because I don't have to keep those little hurts in my memory as a result of your love. Thank you that I can do this quickly, readily, and freely, as it is the way you forgave me.

Out of Wickedness

Let love be without hypocrisy. Abhor what is evil. Cling to what is good. Be kindly affectionate to one another with brotherly love, in honor giving preference to one another; not lagging in diligence, fervent in spirit, serving the Lord.

ROMANS 12:9-11

I hate evil! Father, I love you for putting in my heart such a dislike for the things of the devil and for allowing me to hate that which is wrong. Thank you that I can stand for the good in this world! Father, in this world I can sincerely love others with brotherly affection because of you. I adore you; I hate and loathe everything that is evil or ungodly. I turn in absolute horror from wickedness! I used to love wickedness, and I thank you for delivering me from that love! I prefer others and am diligent, fervent in spirit, serving the Lord!

Love Your Neighbor

For the commandments, "You shall not commit adultery, You shall not murder, You shall not steal, You shall not covet," and any other commandment, are summed up in this word: "You shall love your neighbor as yourself."

ROMANS 13:9 ESV

I love you, Father, because you give me the power to live the way you want me to, without wanting to harm or cheat or steal from my neighbors. Thank you, Father. You have wrapped up very neatly all the commandments in this one statement: to love your neighbor as yourself. Thank you, Father. I can love my neighbors because of you.

A God Pleaser

For do I now persuade men, or God? Or do
I seek to please men? For if I still pleased
men, I would not be a servant of Christ.

GALATIANS 1:10

I praise your holy name, Father, because you haven't
called me to please people but to please you. Thank
you, Father. Now my thoughts can be turned toward
you at all times so that I can think about making youyr
heart glad being a servant of Jesus Christ. I thank you
for allowing me to serve and follow Jesus! Glory! I
don't have to go along with the crowd and do things
I don't want to do because I'm afraid of what they
might think about me! I'm your willing, happy, and
contented servant!

No Evil

They must not slander anyone and must avoid quarreling. Instead, they should be gentle and show true humility to everyone.

TITUS 3:2, NLT

Father, let the words of my mouth be acceptable in your sight! Let me be filled with so much of your love that my tongue will only have words that are sweet as honey. I will bridle my tongue and let no words that are harmful, hurtful, injurious, malignant, disastrous, or ruinous come out of my mouth. My lips shall speak words of love, bringing strength, hope, and cheer to others. I will not gossip, criticize, complain, or manufacture untruths about anyone. Instead I will keep my conversation full of your love!

One Accord

Then make me truly happy by agreeing
wholeheartedly with each other, loving
one another, and working together with
one mind and purpose.

PHILIPPIANS 2:2

Father, I am filling up with your love so my joy
can be complete. I am living in harmony with others
and am of the same mind and one in purpose. I will
have abundant love for all my brothers and sisters in
Christ. I am working toward a unity with people who
are different than me so that strife, selfishness, and
contentiousness will cease. I will love those whose
doctrines do not exactly agree with mine. If they love
Jesus and if we are like-minded in that area, we can be
in one accord and one mind. Let the little, unimportant
things fall by the wayside and let us dwell on the
things that last. Thank you for giving me a love that is
big enough to encompass doctrinal differences. I'm
running over with love! It's splashing on everyone I run
into and it blesses everyone it falls on because of your
love!

The Law of Love

Love suffers long and is kind; love does
not envy; love does not parade itself, is
not puffed up; does not behave rudely,
does not seek its own, is not provoked,
thinks no evil.

1 CORINTHIANS 13:4-5

Father, thank you for this love chapter in the Bible.
Thank you for telling me exactly what love is. Lord, I
will not envy, behave rudely, or seek my own will. Your
wonderful love is flowing through me to reach others.
I will not be irritable or touchy. Thank you, Father, all
of this is only possible because of your love! I praise
you that I don't have to insist on my "rights" and
having my own way. I lost my grudges at the altar of
salvation and I will think no evil of anyone.

JUNE 28

Three Remain

And now abide faith, hope, love, these
three; but the greatest of these is love.

1 CORINTHIANS 13:13

I praise you, Father, for faith, hope, and love. I will
abide in each. Thank you that the greatest one of
these is love. Without love, it would be difficult to have
faith and hope. But with your love, as it is the greatest
of all, we also have faith and hope. We have faith in the
knowledge that Jesus Christ is coming back and hope
that it is going to be soon. We love you because of the
joyful and confident expectation of eternal salvation.
Thank you that you enable us to have true affection
and love for you and for others in this world!

Empowered by Promises

Now hope does not disappoint, because the love of God has been poured out in our hearts by the Holy Spirit who was given to us.

ROMANS 5:5

Father, I thank you because the love in my human heart is not something I have to try to work up. I can spread your love all over the world because you have poured out this amazing love in my heart by the Holy Spirit. Your love is a beautiful gift you give to your children. Thank you, Father, that the world can see your love in me. I don't have to have unbelief or distrust, which would cause me to waver about whether or not I could really love someone. Instead, I am empowered by my faith in you and your promises!

JUNE 30

More than Conquerors

> But in all these things we overwhelmingly
> conquer through Him who loved us.
>
> ROMANS 8:37, NASB

Glory to God, I'm more than a conqueror! Father, how I praise you for that word *all*! Thank you for letting me know that I win *all* the battles because of your love. The same love that allowed Jesus Christ to die on a cross for me makes me more than a conqueror in *all* areas of my life. I don't have to bow to the devil in any area because you've said in *all* these things I am more than a conqueror through Him who loved me. Thank you, Father, for another month of victory in Jesus! Thank you that I always have a surpassing victory in everything because of your great love!

JULY

Freedom from Fear

As you make these declarations, we believe that you will be delivered from the bondage of fear and be totally and completely liberated by declaring God's powerful Word. May the Holy Spirit fill you with His perfect and eternal love, which casts out all fear.

Strong and Courageous

And David said to his son Solomon,
"Be strong and of good courage, and
do it; do not fear nor be dismayed, for
the Lord God—my God—will be with you.
He will not leave you nor forsake you,
until you have finished all the work for the
service of the house of the Lord.

1 CHRONICLES 28:20

Today I'm strong, courageous, and afraid of nothing.
Thank you, Father, because you care about every little
detail of my life. I am not frightened by the size of any
task. You always are with me. I praise you, Father, that
you are with me as I finish the work you have given me
to do. Thank you that I don't have to live the Christian
life in my own strength, but instead, I can rest in you
and be strengthened and assured the work I do turns
out right because you are backing me up all the way!

Bold as a Lion

The wicked flee when no one pursues, but
the righteous are bold as a lion.

PROVERBS 28:1

Today I am bold, bold, *bold!* Father, I praise you for
giving me the boldness of a lion! Thank you for the
righteousness that comes from you. I act and make
decisions with the courage that comes from knowing
you are with me in all I do. I stand up and boldly face all
that comes before me in life. The wicked flee because
they're afraid that what they've done will catch up
with them and destroy them. I don't have to always be
looking over my shoulder in fear as the wicked do. I'm
always on the winning side! I can go into any situation
of the devil's making, and the wicked will flee before
me because you've made me bold as a lion!

A Sound Mind

For God has not given us a spirit of fear, but of power and of love and of a sound mind.

2 TIMOTHY 1:7

I have a sound mind at all times because I have the mind of Christ! I love you, praise you, and thank you, Father because you haven't given me a spirit of fear. I rejoice because fear is never from you. Because you have given me power over the devil and all his doings, I can boldly dismiss any thoughts or feelings of fear that come before me. Thank you, Father, that you've given me a sound mind and the power to face any situation and be victorious in it!

JULY 4

Abundant Life

The thief does not come except to steal, and to kill, and to destroy. I have come that they may have life, and that they may have it more abundantly.

JOHN 10:10

Father, I praise you for the day you granted freedom to this nation. But more than that, I thank you for the freedom and abundance of life you have granted me through your Son, Jesus Christ, who came to defeat the devil and all his evil and destructive ways. Jesus came to free me from the bondage of the devil's fear so that the devil can never again steal the blessings of life from me or my children. Jesus is the way, the truth, and the life, and through Him I have the abundant life you want all your children to have!

Over the Enemy

Behold, I give you the authority to trample
on serpent and scorpion, and over all the
power of the enemy, and nothing shall by
any means hurt you.

LUKE 10:19

Father, you have given me the power to tread on
all the works of the devil without harm coming to me!
I rejoice that you've turned the tables on the devil.
Now I have power over all the power of the enemy,
and he has to run from me! I praise you for making me
immune to the poison of the enemy. I am triumphant
in times of trouble and at peace in the midst of strife.
Thank you, Father, for making me a spiritual warrior so
I can stomp on the works of the enemy wherever I find
them!

Roll Your Works

Commit to the LORD whatever you do, and
he will establish your plans.

PROVERBS 16:3, NIV

Father, I place all my cares, worries, and defeats
into your arms! I commit them to you and trust that
you will take care of them completely. I'm not going
to worry about them any more! I thank you that all my
thoughts are becoming agreeable to your will, and I
will not meditate on what will be unpleasing to you.
I turn my back on all the lusts of the flesh and roll my
works upon you. I hear your voice and do only the
works you tell me to do. I'm excited because I now
have complete assurance that everything I do is going
to be established and succeed. How I praise you that
you make no plans for failure in your Word!

JULY 7

Still Waters

The LORD is my shepherd; I shall not want.
He makes me to lie down in green pastures;
He leads me beside the still waters.

PSALM 23:1-2

I love and praise you, Father, because in the abiding love and care you pour upon me, I fear no evil. With you as my shepherd, I'm surrounded by your protective power at all times. I rejoice that I can relax and enjoy your green pastures and still waters. Wherever you lead me, I have complete trust that all my needs are met. I thank you, Father, for seeing to it that I lack nothing. I praise you because I can look to you for everything I need in my life without worry because you always provide for me. Thank you, Father.

Good Courage

Be strong and of good courage, do
not fear nor be afraid of them; for
the LORD your God, He is the One who
goes with you. He will not leave you nor
forsake you.

DEUTERONOMY 31:6

Father, I'm strong! I'm courageous! I praise you
because I'm not afraid. You are with me in all your
power and glory and righteousness, and nothing
can withstand your might! I give thanks that you are
the Lord my God who never fails me or leaves me no
matter what kind of difficulty or challenge I have to
face. You are the strength in my soul and the courage
in my heart and I fear nothing. Hallelujah! I'm blessed
with victory!

No Fear

The LORD is my light and my salvation; Whom shall I fear? The LORD is the strength of my life; Of whom shall I be afraid? When the wicked came against me to eat up my flesh, my enemies and foes, they stumbled and fell. Though an army may encamp against me, my heart shall not fear; Though war may rise against me, in this I will be confident.

PSALM 27:1-3

Thank you, Father, for shining your light on the path of righteousness so I can see to walk in your ways. I will not fear anyone or anything! You are my strength and my shield. I fear neither the wickedness of my enemies nor the tricks of the devil because you will cause them to stumble and fall. In the midst of the battle I will be confident in you and your love for me. Hallelujah!

His Secret Place

For in the time of trouble He shall hide me
in His pavilion; in the secret place of His
tabernacle He shall hide me; He shall set
me high upon a rock.

PSALM 27:5

I rejoice, Father, that you protect and hide me from
any kind of trouble that comes my way! Thank you
that you always hide me in your pavilion or in the
secret of your tabernacle where the wicked dare not
follow. How I bless and praise you, Father. No matter
what deceitful schemes the devil comes up with to
disrupt my life, you take me out of harm's way and set
me upon a rock where he can't touch me! I love you,
Father!

Looking Up

And now my head shall be lifted up above
my enemies all around me; Therefore I
will offer sacrifices of joy in His tabernacle;
I will sing, yes, I will sing praises to the
LORD.

PSALM 27:6

Father, I praise you because I don't have to look up
at my enemies. You lift my head above them so that
I'm seeing from your perspective! You are the God
of deliverance and the God of my salvation. I offer
sacrifices of joy to you in celebration of the wonderful
way you take care of me! I'm singing praises to you
because you lift me above the trials and tribulations of
the world. I love you with all my heart!

Freedom from Death

There is therefore now no condemnation for those who are in Christ Jesus. For the law of the Spirit of life has set you free in Christ Jesus from the law of sin and death.

ROMANS 8:1-2, ESV

How I praise you, Father, that there is no condemnation or fear in my life. I rejoice because I am in Jesus Christ and I walk after the Spirit! Thank you for the promises in your Word that say that all my sins are forgiven. You don't even remember them, so I don't have any fear of the past. I praise you, Father, that by the law of the Spirit of life in Jesus, I'm free from the law of sin and death. So everything before me and everything in my future is blessed! Hallelujah!

Wherever You Go

This is my command—be strong
and courageous! Do not be afraid or
discouraged. For the LORD your God is
with you wherever you go.

JOSHUA 1:9, NLT

How I thank you, Father, the power and truth of
your commandment make me strong and fill me with
courage! Fear and dismay have no part in my life
because my strength is in you, and I trust you in all
things. When the devil comes against me, I am brave
and jubilant for I know you are with me every moment
day and night, and I have victory over all the power
of darkness! Thank you, Father, that you are with me
wherever I go!

My Salvation

"Behold, God is my salvation, I will trust and not be afraid; For the LORD GOD is my strength and song, And He has become my salvation." Therefore you will joyously draw water from the springs of salvation.

ISAIAH 12:2-3, NASB

Father, I rejoice that you are my salvation! Because of this, I place my whole trust in you and I am never afraid or anxious in anything. I rejoice in you because you are my strength and my song, and with so much confidence and happiness bubbling through me, I sing your praises everywhere I go. Father, I thank you for the wells of your salvation. Your living water renews, blesses, and refreshes my life, giving me such joy that I feel like telling everyone I meet what a glorious God you are!

Priceless Blessing

Inasmuch then as the children have partaken of flesh and blood, He Himself likewise shared in the same, that through death He might destroy him who had the power of death, that is, the devil, and release those who through fear of death were all their lifetime subject to bondage.

HEBREWS 2:14-15

Thank you, Jesus, for taking death upon yourself to destroy the one who had the power of death. Thank you because I'm free of the fear of death and the desperate hunger for power, money, and the things of this world that come from fearing death. I praise you, Father, that Jesus delivered me from sin, the devil, and bondage to fear by shedding His blood for me upon the cross. I thank you for that glorious promise of eternal life in your kingdom! Because death couldn't hold Jesus in the grave, it won't hold me either. I'm rejoicing because my eternal home is with you! Thank you, Father, for the priceless blessing of eternal life!

Perfect in Love

There is no fear in love; but perfect love casts out fear, because fear involves torment. But he who fears has not been made perfect in love.

1 JOHN 4:18

I praise and thank you, glorious Father. Your perfect love flows through me in such great measure that it has cast out fear of any kind and all kinds! I thank you, Father, for removing the torment of fear from my life, for torment comes from the devil, and he has to run from the power of your perfect love! I'm blessed beyond my wildest dreams, Father, because I'm being perfected in your wonderful love!

Ultimate Refuge

God is our refuge and strength, a very present help in trouble. Therefore we will not fear, though the earth be removed, and though the mountains be carried into the midst of the sea; though its waters roar and be troubled, though the mountains shake with its swelling. Selah.

PSALM 46:1-3

Father, I thank and praise you because you are my refuge and strength. You are my help at the moment trouble comes. You are the God of my salvation and you will take care of me no matter what happens. Father, I praise you because you are the Creator, the God of everything, and for that reason, I don't fear anything. Whether the world falls apart or a great earthquake rocks the mountains, I'll be saved and protected by your loving power! Hallelujah!

Walk in Your Ways

In God, whose word I praise, in the LORD, whose word I praise—in God I trust and am not afraid. What can man do to me? I am under vows to you, my God; I will present my thank offerings to you. For you have delivered me from death and my feet from stumbling, that I may walk before God in the light of life.

PSALM 56:10-13, NIV

Father, I trust you so much that there's no room in my life for fear! I love your promises for you always keep them, and I thank you for all the help you've given me. I thank you for saving me from death and for keeping my feet from slipping so I can walk in your ways. Father, I rejoice in your light!

Shadow of God

He who dwells in the shelter of the Most High will abide in the shadow of the Almighty. I will say to the LORD, "My refuge and my fortress, my God, in whom I trust."

PSALM 91:1-2

I thank you, Father, because I abide in the safety and comfort of your shadow where no evil can touch me. You are my refuge and my fortress, and I thank you and praise you that you are a God who keeps all His promises to His children. My trust is always fulfilled in you. Because I dwell in the secret place of the highest, the devil can't make fear fall upon me. Instead, I am lifted up and blessed over and over by the love and power with which you surround me!

No Plague

No evil shall befall you, nor shall any
plague come near your dwelling; for He
shall give His angels charge over you, to
keep you in all your ways.

PSALM 91:10-11

Father, thank you that no evil can befall me, and no
plague or sickness can come near my house because
you said so! Thank you that I don't have to worry
about these things any more. You send your angels
and charge them to take care of me in every way! I
praise you, Father, for loving me so much that your
angels stick by me night and day to guard and protect
me, my house, and family from everything the devil
might try to do to us. Thank you, Father, that your
Word frees me from fear of sickness, calamity, and
disease! Hallelujah!

Winning Again

> Then he said to me, "This is the word of
> the Lord to Zerubbabel: Not by might,
> nor by power, but by my Spirit, says the
> Lord of hosts."
>
> ZECHARIAH 4:6

Thank you, Father, that I don't have to have fear.
You've promised that I don't have to win battles in my
own strength or power, but instead, you will win them
for me by your Spirit! Glory to the Lord of hosts! Here I
am, winning again!

Trust in the Lord

Whoever gives heed to instruction prospers, and blessed is the one who trusts in the LORD.

PROVERBS 16:20, NIV

I love to receive your blessings, Father, because I know that everything that comes from you is good! I obey you without hesitation because everything you tell me to do comes from your righteousness, and I rejoice in your righteousness. I have no fear, nervousness, worry, or care about the future or about problems because your blessings are upon me. I'm happy and I'm singing your praises because I put my trust, my faith, my confidence, and my hope in you. I'm full of anticipation for the good things in life, and fear went out the window when faith and trust came in!

Almighty Wisdom

The LORD by wisdom founded the earth, by understanding He established the heavens. By His knowledge the deeps were broken up and the skies drip with dew. My son, let them not vanish from your sight; Keep sound wisdom and discretion, so they will be life to your soul and adornment to your neck. Then you will walk in your way securely and your foot will not stumble. When you lie down, you will not be afraid; When you lie down, your sleep will be sweet. Do not be afraid of sudden fear nor of the onslaught of the wicked when it comes; For the LORD will be your confidence and will keep your foot from being caught.

PROVERBS 3:19-26, NASB

Father, your wisdom that founded the earth is the same wisdom that guides my life and guards me from fear of falling or stumbling. You are my confidence and by your wisdom and knowledge there is life in my soul and grace in my life. Father, I am awed by the magnificent miracle of your creation, and my sleep is sweet because I am protected day and night by your mighty power! Hallelujah!

JULY 24

Always Faithful

The fear of man brings a snare, but
whoever trusts in the LORD shall be safe.

PROVERBS 29:25

I thank you, Father, for taking all fear from me. Fear
is just an invitation for the devil to take advantage
with one of his deceitful snares. I love and praise you,
Father, for being the God I can trust with all my heart.
I do trust you because you are always faithful to keep
your children safe and filled with blessings. You are
wonderful to me!

Wonderful Miracles

And Moses said to the people, "Do not be afraid. Stand still, and see the salvation of the Lord, which He will accomplish for you today. For the Egyptians whom you see today, you shall see again no more forever. The Lord will fight for you, and you shall hold your peace." And the Lord said to Moses, "Why do you cry to Me? Tell the children of Israel to go forward."

EXODUS 14:13-15

Father, thank you for the simple, direct, and powerful ways you deliver us from seemingly hopeless situations. No situation is hopeless before your mighty power. I move forward in Jesus' name through every difficulty. You are fighting for me and I will be at peace. You are a God of wonderful miracles and faithfulness to your people!

Fear Not

Don't be afraid, for I am with you. Don't
be discouraged, for I am your God. I will
strengthen you and help you. I will hold
you up with my victorious right hand. See,
all your angry enemies lie there, confused
and humiliated. Anyone who opposes
you will die and come to nothing. You
will look in vain for those who tried to
conquer you. Those who attack you will
come to nothing. For I hold you by your
right hand—I, the LORD your God. And I
say to you, "Don't be afraid. I am here to
help you. Though you are a lowly worm,
O Jacob, don't be afraid, people of Israel,
for I will help you. I am the LORD, your
Redeemer. I am the Holy One of Israel."

ISAIAH 41:10-14, NLT

I am thankful, Father, that you bring your people to
victory no matter what the situation. Your right hand
is more powerful than all the armies of the world with
all their weapons, and no one can stand against me
because you are for me! Thank you, Father, that I am
victorious in all situations!

Rescue Me

But now, thus says the LORD, who created
you, O Jacob, and He who formed you,
O Israel: "Fear not, for I have redeemed
you; I have called you by your name;
You are Mine. When you pass through the
waters, I will be with you; And through the
rivers, they shall not overflow you. When
you walk through the fire, you shall not be
burned, nor shall the flame scorch you.

ISAIAH 43:1-2

How I praise you, Father, for redeeming me, calling
me by name, rescuing me from trouble, difficulty, and
oppression, and saving me! Glorious Father, I rejoice
that you openly declare in your Word that I am yours!
Wherever I go—East, West, North or South —you call
me to yourself because you love me. Because you are
with me, I don't fear deep water, fire, or all the power
of the devil for you will rescue me from all of them!
Father, I praise you and thank you for who you are!

Rid of Worries

Do not be afraid of those who kill the body but cannot kill the soul. Rather, be afraid of the One who can destroy both soul and body in hell. Are not two sparrows sold for a penny? Yet not one of them will fall to the ground outside your Father's care. And even the very hairs of your head are all numbered. So don't be afraid; you are worth more than many sparrows.

MATTHEW 10:28-31, NIV

How exciting, Father, to know that you love me so much you have even numbered the hairs on my head! Not only do you know those I have, you know those I have lost. I don't fear any person on this earth because you notice when the smallest bird falls to the ground. You always know when I need your help, and instantly, you are right there with me. I praise you, Father, for getting rid of all my worries because you love me so much! I'm certainly glad to be worth more to you than a sparrow!

Everlasting Arms

The eternal God is your refuge, and
underneath are the everlasting arms; He
will thrust out the enemy from before you,
and will say, "Destroy!"

DEUTERONOMY 33:27

Father, I give praise to you for being the eternal God
who has complete power over all things past, present,
and future. I thank you for forgiving all my sins of the
past, loving me right now, and giving me a wonderful
future to look forward to! I praise you for holding me
with love in your everlasting arms. You are my refuge,
and nothing can harm me regardless of the situation.
Thank you for always going before me in your glory
and power so that the wicked are thrust out of my
path. Father, I love your everlasting arms!

Ultimate Winner

What you decide on will be done, and light
will shine on your ways.

JOB 22:28, NIV

Bless you, Father, that I don't have to worry about
whether or not I'm going to be a failure or a success.
Your blueprint for my life makes it so simple. I'm
throwing fear out the window because you've said
that what I decide on will be done. How I praise you.
I'm walking in the light of your favor, and it's shining
upon my ways! Father, what a privilege to be able to
follow your Word so easily and know that you make us
winner all the time. I love you for that!

Prayerful Peace

Do not be anxious about anything, but in every situation, by prayer and petition, with thanksgiving, present your requests to God. And the peace of God, which transcends all understanding, will guard your hearts and your minds in Christ Jesus.

PHILIPPIANS 4:6-7, NIV

How I thank and praise you, Father, because I don't need to worry about anything. Your love for me is so great that I am filled with and surrounded by your mighty power at all times. Because of your promises and your Word, I have peace in all circumstances. Your peace surpasses all understanding. It is a peace that guards my heart and mind in Christ Jesus. I praise you for the wonderful blessing of that peace! Hallelujah!

August

Strength

August is the time when energy can start to drag because of the long, hot, summer days. Thank God for His Word that declares: "*But those who wait on the Lord shall renew their strength; They shall mount up with wings like eagles, they shall run and not be weary, they shall walk and not faint*" (Isaiah 40:31).

Let's mount up with wings as eagles and soar higher this month than we ever have. Declare these Scriptures four and five times every day!

Whether these Scriptures are new or familiar, remind yourself of what God has for you in order to make you stronger in your daily life.

Why not select at least two Scripture verses this month to memorize? Say them out loud or in your thoughts every day, as often as they come to your mind.

Mouth of God

Jesus answered, "It is written: 'Man shall not live on bread alone, but on every word that comes from the mouth of God.'"

MATTHEW 4:4

Father, I thank you because I don't have to exist only on earthly food. I live in an eternal realm and my most delicious meals and desserts are the words that come out of your mouth! Thank you, Father, that your Word is true, and everything you have said will come to pass because you spoke it. You are a God who cannot lie. Thank you that I don't have to depend just on meat and potatoes for strength, but I can depend on you from whom our real strength comes! Thank you for saying, "It is written," because the devil has to run when I say those words to him!

Testimony Over Death

> And they overcame him by the blood
> of the Lamb and by the word of their
> testimony, and they did not love their lives
> to the death.
>
> REVELATION 12:11

Thank you, Father, because the blood of the Lamb overcomes all things and makes us overcomers! I praise you, Father, because the blood of Jesus was shed for each and every one of us, and this blood is more powerful than the devil. He trembles when he comes close to the bloodline that surrounds us! The very word of my testimony gives me power over all of the enemy! Thank you, Father, that when I speak your Word, it becomes my word, and is power!

Good News

The Spirit of the Lord is upon me, because he has anointed me to proclaim good news to the poor. He has sent me to proclaim liberty to the captives and recovering of sight to the blind, to set at liberty those who are oppressed.

LUKE 4:18, ESV

Father, how I bless you that because I'm a joint heir with Jesus, this promise is mine. The Spirit of the Lord is upon me and I know what I am to do. I share the good news, love the brokenhearted who feel that nobody loves them. I speak your words of deliverance to those who are captive and slaves to habits of the flesh. I praise you that your anointing is here at all times whether I feel it or not. Thank you for giving me such an exciting job!

Whatever Things

Finally, brethren, whatever things
are true, whatever things are noble,
whatever things are just, whatever things
are pure, whatever things are lovely,
whatever things are of good report, if
there is any virtue and if there is anything
praiseworthy—meditate on these things.

PHILIPPIANS 4:8

Father, I praise you because I don't have to think
on the evil things of the devil. I don't have to worry
about the problems of the world and the crises that
arise. I don't have to be disturbed or tormented
because I follow your instructions and think on
uplifting things, which are true, honest, just, pure, and
lovely. I meditate upon all that is good, virtuous, and
praiseworthy. I fix my eyes on you and these things,
Father.

Spiritual Swords

We use God's mighty weapons, not worldly weapons, to knock down the strongholds of human reasoning and to destroy false arguments. We destroy every proud obstacle that keeps people from knowing God. We capture their rebellious thoughts and teach them to obey Christ.

2 CORINTHIANS 10:4-5, NLT

Thank you, Father, that my weapons are not of this world. They are spiritual and powerful because they come from you. You do not expect me to use carnal weapons; you give me the mighty sword of your Spirit, which is the Word of God. I cast down my vain imaginations, which the devil would like to put into my mind. I bring all of my thoughts to the wonderful obedience of Christ because of your mighty power! All rebellious thoughts will obey Christ and my mind will be fixed upon Him.

Every Word

Do not let any unwholesome talk come out of your mouths, but only what is helpful for building others up according to their needs, that it may benefit those who listen.

EPHESIANS 4:29, NIV

Father, how I praise you for instructing what should come out of my mouth. Thank you for telling me that I shouldn't mock, ridicule, deny truth, confuse, or speak corruption in any way. Words that don't edify and minister grace to others do not glorify you. I will not complain, criticize, or use unwholesome and worthless talk. I praise you that every word will be used to glorify you at all times so that it may benefit all who listen.

Heavenly Vitamins

They who wait for the LORD shall renew their strength; they shall mount up with wings like eagles; they shall run and not be weary; they shall walk and not faint.

ISAIAH 40:31, ESV

Today I feel like flying! I rejoice and thank you, Father, for the supernatural power and energy you give me. When I serve and wait upon you, I can mount up like an eagle and draw close to you, as the eagles draw close to the sun. When I run, I'm not weary, and when I walk, I don't faint. Even when I'm tired, you give me the extra boost of energy, strength, and vigor I need. When my enthusiasm begins to lag and my zeal begins to fade, you're right there with those heavenly vitamins. I'm running with no weariness and walking joyfully and upright!

Divine Rest

Come to Me, all you who labor and are heavy laden, and I will give you rest. Take My yoke upon you and learn from Me, for I am gentle and lowly in heart, and you will find rest for your souls.

MATTHEW 11:28-29

I'm so rested, Father. Thank you for the privilege of knowing that when I am faced with problems, I can come to Jesus and He will give me rest. Thank you, Father, that your burden is light, and when I take your yoke upon me, I have joyful rest in you. I praise you because you are always gentle and there to take my burdens from me. How I praise you that your yoke is wholesome and good and not harsh, hard, sharp, or pressing. Instead, it remains comfortable, gracious, and pleasant! Bless you for that divine rest!

Beyond Dreams

Call to Me, and I will answer you, and show you great and mighty things, which you do not know.

JEREMIAH 33:3

I want to see more and more! I love you, Father, for always answering me when I call! Thank you that in answer to my call you will show me great and mighty things, which I don't even know about! You show me the supernatural and new understanding about who you are each day. I'm calling and will continue to call because I want to see your glory and your power more than I ever have before. I delight in and want you to show me things beyond my wildest dreams or imagination.

Filled with Glory

But truly, as I live, all the earth shall be
filled with the glory of the LORD.

NUMBERS 14:21

Father, I want to see your glory! I want to bask in the
magnificence of your presence, and I can hardly wait
to see the entire earth filled with your glory! I want to
see the whole earth filled with your saints who are full
of glory and joy. Great is the glory of the Lord. I thank
you that you are a sun and shield, and you give grace
and glory! Father, you are a shield for me, my glory,
and the lifter of my head! I bless you that even though
darkness covers the earth, your glory shall be seen on
us!

Flee Away

So the ransomed of the LORD shall return, and come to Zion with singing, with everlasting joy on their heads. They shall obtain joy and gladness; sorrow and sighing shall flee away.

ISAIAH 51:11

I'm redeemed by the blood of the Lamb! I thank you that I can sing all the time because your everlasting joy is always pouring upon my head. I thank you that this is an everlasting joy that will never fade away. How I praise you. You don't give me sorrow and sadness, but instead, you give me joy, joy, *joy!* I love you because sorrow and mourning are fleeing away from my life, just as you have promised. How I love you and praise you for all the promises that are mine!

Steps of Good Men

The steps of a man are established by
the LORD, when he delights in his way.

PSALM 37:23, ESV

Father, I rejoice that I'm walking in the steps you
have ordered. Thank you that you direct each and
every step I take. I don't have to worry about the
direction I'm going. I'm walking exactly where you
tell me to walk. I rejoice because the way you direct
my steps is sure and true, superior to anything I could
do to find my own way. I'm delighted because it
doesn't make any difference if I'm going east, west,
north or south. You keep my footsteps going in the
right direction. I praise you because you aren't only
interested in my entire trip, but you're interested in
every single step I take!

Special Gift

Do not neglect the gift that is in you, which was given to you by prophecy with the laying on of the hands of the eldership. Meditate on these things; give yourself entirely to them, that your progress may be evident to all.

1 TIMOTHY 4:14-15

Father, I praise you because the Holy Spirit gave me that special, inward gift. I am practicing, cultivating, and meditating on all these things so that your grace may be evident to all. I am not going to neglect the helps you have given me to live the Christian life or to minister in the life of someone else, but I am stirring them up. I give myself entirely to you and the gifts that you've placed within me. I am a blessing to all.

Strength and Power

God is my strength and power, and He
makes my way perfect.

2 SAMUEL 22:33

Father, how I praise you that you are my strength
and my power. I am not satisfied with the things of
this world and my own strength because you have
given me your very own strength and power. Father,
thank you for being willing to make my way perfect.
The energy I have comes from the mighty energy that
Jesus Christ puts in me, energizing and empowering
me to do what He wants me to do. Thank you that you
are my strong fortress and because you guide me, you
set me free! Thank you, Father!

Power to Weak

He gives power to the weak, and to those
who have no might He increases strength.

ISAIAH 40:29

Father, I love you even during my weaknesses and
faults. I will not rely on my own abilities, so I put my
whole trust in you! Thank you for the power that you
give to me when I'm weak and faint. When I'm worn
out and undone, you cause me to not look to myself
and my solutions. You increase my strength, causing it
to multiply and abound. Even in my darkest moments,
you continually charge and recharge my spiritual
batteries with supernatural strength! I worship you for
this, Father!

Blessings and Benefits

Blessed be the Lord, who daily loads us
with benefits, the God of our salvation!

PSALM 68:19

I praise you, love you, and worship you, Father,
for giving me so many benefits day after day. Your
blessings are not a one-time thing, but instead, you
daily load me down with all your wonderful benefits,
promises, and blessings. You are a river to me! I bless
you, the God of my salvation! As I look over this day,
Father, I praise you because you don't just give me a
little sampling of benefits. I'm excited that you have
an overabundance of everything. You load me and
continue to load me with your blessings and benefits!

Perfect Peace

You will keep him in perfect peace, whose
mind is stayed on You, because he trusts
in You.

ISAIAH 26:3

How I love and adore you, Father, because my heart,
my mind, and my soul have perfect and constant
peace. Your Word says that if I keep my mind on you
and trust, peace is mine. Jesus, you are the Prince of
Peace and I fix my eyes upon you. I don't lean on my
own understanding. Instead I lean on your trustworthy
ways and I hope in you. Thank you that my mind can
confidently and continually stay on you!

Forever Home

Do not let your hearts be troubled. You believe in God; believe also in me. My Father's house has many rooms; if that were not so, would I have told you that I am going there to prepare a place for you? And if I go and prepare a place for you, I will come back and take you to be with me that you also may be where I am.

JOHN 14:1-3, NIV

Thank you, Jesus, for giving me an untroubled heart. I believe in you and your great love for me. You are preparing a place for me where you are. I am excited to think about what you are building. It is magnificent and far beyond what I can imagine. I look forward to your return so that I can be with you forever. Thank you, Jesus, for giving me such an exciting future!

Blind Given Sight

I will bring the blind by a way they did not know; I will lead them in paths they have not known. I will make darkness light before them, and crooked places straight. These things I will do for them, and not forsake them.

ISAIAH 42:16

Once I was blind, but now I see. Even before you saved me, you directed my footsteps so that I would go down paths to lead me to you. I praise you that my steps are ordered by the Lord, and you turn the darkness inside out and make it light. You take the most crooked path imaginable and straighten it out. You are doing this for me because you love me. Father, I praise you for your total protection at all times.

Perfect Lamb

"This is the covenant that I will make with them after those days," says the LORD: "I will put My laws into their hearts, and in their minds I will write them," then He adds, "Their sins and their lawless deeds I will remember no more."

HEBREWS 10:16-17

Father, how I praise you. Your offering of your perfect Lamb has completely cleansed me! I love you for putting your laws right into my heart and writing them into my mind. I don't depend only on memorizing words from the law because your Holy Spirit reminds me of them constantly. Father, I love you for forgiving and forgetting all my sins and iniquities. I praise you that I don't have to remember them either because you have forgotten them!

AUGUST 21

He Hears

The righteous cry out, and the LORD hears,
and delivers them out of all their troubles.

PSALM 34:17

Lord, I see that you are so very good. When I cry out for help, you are there to deliver me at all times. I magnify the Lord, and I exalt your holy name. You always hear me. You have no hearing problems and your ears are tuned to the righteous at all times. Even though many evils confront me, you deliver me out of all of them. You redeem the life of your servants, and none who take refuge in you shall be condemned or held guilty! Thank you for being my deliverer!

Generations to Come

"As for me, this is my covenant with
them," says the LORD. "My Spirit, who
is on you, will not depart from you, and
my words that I have put in your mouth
will always be on your lips, on the lips
of your children and on the lips of their
descendants—from this time on and
forever," says the LORD.

ISAIAH 59:21, NIV

Father, I thank you for the covenant you gave to
me. I thank you for the words that you have put in
my mouth. I praise you that your words shall not
depart out of my mouth, nor out of the mouths of my
children, nor out of the mouths of my grandchildren.
Thank you, Father, for not only blessing me personally,
but also for blessing me down through all generations
that follow me. I praise you that their hearts will be
so in tune with you that their mouths will be pure and
speak your words at all times. I love you, Father, for
this wonderful promise.

Coming Light

Arise, shine; for your light has come! And the glory of the LORD is risen upon you.

ISAIAH 60:1

Father, thank you for Jesus, the light of the world, who lives in me. I praise you because I don't have to lie down and wallow in misery, but I arise from the depression and discouragement in which circumstances have kept me. You constantly let your light shine through me. I thank you that I have risen to a new life, and I am radiant with the glory of the Lord. Your glory is risen upon me! I can't see it, but I praise you that the world can— just because you said so!

AUGUST 24

Be Full

These things I have spoken to you, that
My joy may remain in you, and that your
joy may be full.

JOHN 15:11

Father, how I praise you for your words. They are
words of hope, inspiration, assurance, and security
for all the problems of life. Those words have I
hidden in my heart so I might not sin against you.
When I keep them safely tucked away in there to be a
constant reminder to me of your love and perfection
at all times, my joy remains, and my cup of joy is full,
complete, and overflowing. I thank you for this. My joy
is full! It isn't half full. It isn't a quarter full; it's full all
the way up to the top because your Word says so!

Old Nature

So then, brethren, we are under obligation, not to the flesh, to live according to the flesh.

ROMANS 8:12, NASB

How I praise you, Father, that I have absolutely no obligation to my old nature! I don't ever have to do what it tempts me to, and even when my old nature begs me to do something, I don't have to obey it because there are absolutely no obligations left. I am no longer a debtor to my old nature, so I do not have to live a life ruled by the standard set up by the dictates of the flesh. I praise you, Father, because the old way was death, but the new way is life! Hallelujah!

Share with Him

Now if we are children, then we are heirs—heirs of God and co-heirs with Christ, if indeed we share in his sufferings in order that we may also share in his glory.

ROMANS 8:17, NIV

Father, I praise you because I am your child. I am an heir of God and a co-heir with Christ. Thank you because I share your treasures and have everything that you gave to Jesus! Hallelujah! You are so good to me and I love being your child. I am blessed to share in your sufferings and in your glory. This is one of the greatest of all treasures—your abiding, everlasting, continuing, overwhelming, glorious love!

All Parts of Me

One God and Father of all, who is above
all, and through all, and in you all.

EPHESIANS 4:6

Father, how I love you because I don't have to worry
about which God to serve. You are the only true God,
the Father of us all, and you are sovereign above all. I
don't have to worry about whose God is best. You're
living and flowing in every part of me: my eyes, nose,
mouth, ears, arms, hands, fingers, legs, feet, and even
my toes. You are filling all of me afresh with your Spirit
right now, and I thank you, Father.

AUGUST 28

In You

In you, O LORD, I put my trust;
let me never be put to shame.

PSALM 71:1

Praise you, Father; my trust is in you. When problems arise and pressures come, I will not be perplexed because I know you and my trust is in you, in whom there is all wisdom and truth. I thank you, Father, that I don't have to search around and try to find someone whom I can trust, but I am secure in the knowledge of confidently taking refuge in you at all times! I will not be put the shame because I place my trust in you.

All You Do

Do all things without complaining and disputing, that you may become blameless and harmless, children of God without fault in the midst of a crooked and perverse generation, among whom you shine as lights in the world, holding fast the word of life, so that I may rejoice in the day of Christ that I have not run in vain or labored in vain.

PHILIPPIANS 2:14-16

Thank you, Father. I don't have to argue and complain because you've given me a power that keeps me above all of the things of the flesh. Thank you for your instructions on how I can live a clean and innocent life. Father, I thank you that I am a light beaming your love all over the world as I hold out to all people your Word of life. I hold fast to you and will rejoice in the day of Christ because I have run my race well. I look forward to hearing you say, "Well done!"

Unexplainable Promises

He did not waver at the promise of God through unbelief, but was strengthened in faith, giving glory to God, and being fully convinced that what He had promised He was also able to perform.

ROMANS 4:20-21

Father, I praise you that I don't have to waver with doubt at any of your promises. Your promises are exceedingly true and will come to pass. You are strengthening me in faith and I give glory to you. I praise you that your Word is full of promises for me and you will accomplish each and every one of them. I love you, Father, for being a God with whom all things are possible.

Dead to Flesh

We know that our old sinful selves were crucified with Christ so that sin might lose its power in our lives. We are no longer slaves to sin. For when we died with Christ we were set free from the power of sin.

ROMANS 6:6-7, NLT

Father, I praise you that I can go to my own spiritual funeral and see myself dead to sin! I praise you that in our dying to self you have totally and completely removed me from sin. I praise you for the end of self. I love you, Father, for giving me another month of victory and joy. I am no longer a slave and I don't ever have to live in the flesh again! You have set me free from the power of sin. Hallelujah!

September

Healing

Did you know that salvation not only includes the forgiveness of our sins, but also the healing of our bodies? Even if we don't get healed right away, healing is still *for* us. God does not want us sick!

When sickness comes upon us, we know that we can call upon the name of Jesus for healing. The name of Jesus is above every disease that exists!

God has also given us another avenue for healing. In Mark 16:18 the Bible says, *"They will lay hands on the sick, and they will recover."* We can go to a Spirit-filled believer and have them lay hands on us and receive the healing that we need.

Jesus said to the believer, *"Behold, I give you the authority to trample on serpents and scorpions, and over all the power of the enemy, and nothing shall by any means hurt you"* (Luke 10:19). The power was God's and then He gave it to us. This is the reason we can speak with authority when we speak healing over anyone who has been tormented by the devil.

Let's declare our healing right now. We are asking God to anoint this page so when you lay hands on it, you will receive healing!

Divine Health

Bless the LORD, O my soul, and forget
not all His benefits: who forgives all your
iniquities, who heals all your diseases.

PSALM 103:2-3

Father, I praise you for being the God who loves us
so much that you even remind us in your Word not
to forget *all* your benefits! Father, don't ever let me
forget a single one of them because I rejoice with
open arms to receive all the blessings you want me
to have! I thank you that all my sins are gone, gone,
gone. You have healed *all* my diseases. I'm walking in
divine health, and I praise you for that! Thank you for
redeeming my life from the pit of corruption and for
beautifying me with your loving kindness and tender
mercies!

Deliverance

He sent His word and healed them, and
delivered them from their destructions.

PSALM 107:20

Thank you, Father, for sending your Word to heal us.
Thank you that there is no sickness in your kingdom,
and we don't have to be in bondage to disease and
illness. I love you, Father, because the prescription
to heal every disease is written in your Word! We're
delivered from all of our destructions and healed of
all our physical problems. Thank you for sending your
Word of healing and deliverance. Thank you for your
unfailing words of all your good promises—in the past,
the present, and the future! I love you and worship you
for that!

SEPTEMBER 3

Disease-Free

He said, "If you listen carefully to
the LORD your God and do what is right
in his eyes, if you pay attention to his
commands and keep all his decrees, I will
not bring on you any of the diseases I
brought on the Egyptians, for I am
the LORD, who heals you."

EXODUS 15:26, NIV

I'm listening carefully, Father, and I praise you for
talking long enough for me to hear your voice and for
keeping your Holy Spirit constantly after me so that I
will do what is right. Thank you for my ears that hear,
and thank you for the promise that you won't put any
of the diseases of the Egyptians upon me. Thank you,
Lord, you bring good news and healing! I praise you for
being a disease-free God!

SEPTEMBER 4

By His Stripes

But He was wounded for our transgressions, He was bruised for our iniquities; the chastisement for our peace was upon Him, and by His stripes we are healed.

ISAIAH 53:5

I thank you, Father, for your wonderful Word of prophecy through Isaiah, as he predicted the suffering of your Son years before it happened! Thank you for the wounds that covered our transgressions. How I love Jesus for taking the bruises for our iniquities and the chastisement of our peace! Thank you, Jesus, because those stripes on your back were taken for my healing. I am healed because of the miracle of miracles that took place over 2,000 years ago.

Bore Sickness

That it might be fulfilled which was spoken by Isaiah the prophet, saying: "He Himself took our infirmities and bore our sicknesses."

MATTHEW 8:17

How I bless you and praise you, Father, because Jesus took every one of my infirmities, and he accepted all of this sickness upon himself. I praise you, Father, that he didn't leave some of them out, but instead, he took all the sicknesses in the entire world and bore each and every one of them for us. Now don't have to bear sickness because there's no point in both of us having it. I'm not accepting sickness in my body. It has no right here! Jesus' sacrifice was for my complete healing.

SEPTEMBER 6

Health to Flesh

> My son, give attention to my words;
> incline your ear to my sayings. Do not let
> them depart from your eyes; keep them
> in the midst of your heart; for they are life
> to those who find them, and health to all
> their flesh.

PROVERBS 4:20-22

Father, I'm listening! I'm attending to your Word.
I've got my ear turned to you and tuned into you. I've
got my eyes glued to your words, and I'm not going to
let them get out of my sight. I'm feeding on your Word
so it becomes a vital part of me, right in the midst of
my heart! I praise you for the life that you have given
to me through your Word and for the health which I'm
enjoying every day. I thank you, Father!

Dead to Sin

He personally carried our sins in his body
on the cross so that we can be dead
to sin and live for what is right. By his
wounds you are healed.

1 PETER 2:24, NLT

Thank you, Father, for the cross where Jesus died.
He took upon Himself all of our sins so that I don't
have a sin left against me. He took each and every
one of them and bore them so I can live in your
righteousness. How I love you for giving us that health
through those stripes He endured. Now I can say,
"Healing is mine!" with full confidence. Father, I praise
you! I confess these words over and over again, "By
His stripes I was healed! By His stripes I was healed! By
His stripes I was healed!" Hallelujah!

Innermost Prayers

Thus says the LORD, the God of David your
father: "I have heard your prayer, I have
seen your tears; surely I will heal you."

2 KINGS 20:5

Heavenly Father, thank you for looking down at me
and seeing my tears—all of them. I praise you that not
a single one of them has escaped you. Thank you for
your promise to heal me. I love you, Father, from the
innermost recesses of my heart. I thank you because
you have heard my prayers. Whether eloquently
spoken or poorly worded, you hear my prayers and
you will heal me.

All Sickness

And the LORD will take away from you all sickness, and will afflict you with none of the terrible diseases of Egypt which you have known, but will lay them on all those who hate you.

DEUTERONOMY 7:15

Father, I'm healed before I get sick! Hallelujah! I praise you, Father, for taking away from me all illness and disease. You love and protect those who are faithful to you. Thank you, Father, because your Word promises that you take away from me *all sickness* and not just some sicknesses. I rejoice in the wonderful health you have given me, heavenly Father!

A Dose of Laughter

A merry heart does good, like medicine,
but a broken spirit dries the bones.

PROVERBS 17:22

Father, I'm laughing right now! Ha, ha, ha, ho, ho, ho, he, he, he! You said that laughter does me good like a medicine. I thank you for that dose of heavenly medicine, and now I'm going to laugh all day long because a merry heart brings healing like a medicine. Thank you for letting me know that I should have a good sense of humor. Thank you that I don't have to have a depressed mind or a broken spirit, which dries up my bones. You have renewed me! Thank you that we can give my brothers and sisters in Christ a dose of medicine when they need it by cheering their hearts with laughter. Ha, ha, ha, ho, ho, he, he, he!

Be Cleansed

When He had come down from the mountain, great multitudes followed Him. And behold, a leper came and worshiped Him, saying, "Lord, if You are willing, You can make me clean." Then Jesus put out His hand and touched him, saying, "I am willing; be cleansed." Immediately his leprosy was cleansed.

MATTHEW 8:1-3

Jesus, thank you that you are willing to heal me and you are healing me. I love you because you *want* me to have all the good things in life. I bless you because your Word tells me that Jesus has no desire for me to be sick. You want to heal me! I praise you, Father, because you are a God who wants us in perfect and divine health!

Nothing Is Too Hard

Behold, I am the LORD, the God of all flesh.
Is there anything too hard for Me?

JEREMIAH 32:27

Father, you are the God of *all* flesh! I praise you because you never do things halfway; you always go all the way and finish what you started! I love you, Father! I'm so glad that nothing is too hard for you! When my own situations become so big and they overwhelm me, I can give them to you and rest safe and secure in the knowledge that *nothing* is too hard for you. Father, I worship you because my insurmountable mountains are stacks of children's blocks to you that can easily be knocked over. Because of this, I give you all my troubles. Hallelujah!

Here I Am

Then shall your light break forth like the dawn, and your healing shall spring up speedily; your righteousness shall go before you; the glory of the LORD shall be your rear guard. Then you shall call, and the LORD will answer; you shall cry, and he will say, "Here I am."

ISAIAH 58:8-9

Thank you, Father, for the glorious light you shed upon me. I thank you for your promises of healing and restoration. Your godliness leads me forward and your goodness is just like a shield for me, bringing me peace and prosperity. You're always there when I call, and thank you that you so quickly reply, "I am here!" Glory, Father, I'm overcome with your promises! Thank you for removing every form of false and wicked speaking and for guiding me continually!

SEPTEMBER 14

Prolonged Days

The fear of the LORD prolongs days, but
the years of the wicked will be shortened.

PROVERBS 10:27

Heavenly Father, I praise you that my life is long.
I love you and stand in awe of your majesty and
greatness, and because of this, you lengthen my days.
I praise you for shortening the days of the wicked. I
rejoice that I have favor with you. You bless my days
with health and peace of mind. You reward the lives of
the righteous. Thank you for always blessing me with
all the good things in life. I love you!

Wise Tongue

There is one who speaks like the piercings of a sword, but the tongue of the wise promotes health.

PROVERB 12:18

Father, you have given me a wise tongue and have taught me to speak divine health. You've taught me not to let any corrupt communication come out of my mouth and not to acknowledge the sickness of the devil. Instead, I confidently say, "I'm catching a healing," when the devil tries to give me a cold. Father, I praise you because my own tongue brings your health into my life! I bless you for this! I thank you that a wise tongue speaks your Word, which brings healing to my body. Thank you for harnessing my tongue to bring it under control!

Wholesome Tongue

A wholesome tongue is a tree of life, but perverseness in it breaks the spirit.

PROVERBS 15:4

Father, my tongue is wholesome! You are the one who has made this possible. I thank you that my tongue is a tree of life that brings health and happiness. Because you control my tongue, I don't break down my spirit with contrary words. I give up the griping that brings discouragement and speak words that are gentle and have healing power. My tongue is wholesome and brings wholeness into my life. I love you for this, Father.

Many Children

Worship the LORD your God, and his
blessing will be on your food and water.
I will take away sickness from among
you, and none will miscarry or be barren in
your land. I will give you a full life span.

EXODUS 23:25-26

I praise you, Father, that my bread is blessed and
so is my water. I thank you because you have taken
sickness away from me and my family. Women can
stand on your Word and not have miscarriages. The
wombs of your children will not be barren and married
couples that want children will be fruitful. I praise
you, Father, for making the barren woman the joyful
mother of many children and have a full life. Glory!

SEPTEMBER 18

Hide His Words

He also taught me, and said to me: "Let your heart retain my words; Keep my commands, and live."

PROVERBS 4:4

Father, I love you and praise you because your words are written in my heart. I'm keeping them there by memorizing and declaring them, and I know what your Word says. I'm keeping your commandments. Thank you, Father, that your Word has told me if I do this I will have a long and happy life. I'm holding fast to every word you have said. I'm declaring all of your promises, and I'm hiding them in the deepest recesses of my heart so that I won't sin against you, Father! I keep your commandments and I am living abundantly.

SEPTEMBER 19

Divine Bandages

He heals the brokenhearted
and binds up their wounds.

PSALM 147:3

Father, even though my heart has been broken, you put it back together again. Thank you that you didn't leave me to gather up the pieces, but you gathered them all up for me and put them together to make my heart whole again. Your loving care is curing all my pains and all my sorrows. Thank you for those divine bandages with that everlasting healing power in them that you wrap around all of my wounds. Hallelujah, Father, I love you for that!

Raise Him Up

And the prayer of faith will save the sick,
and the Lord will raise him up. And if he
has committed sins, he will be forgiven.

JAMES 5:15

Heavenly Father, thank you because I can pray for
myself, and I can also have others pray for me because
you said the "prayer of faith" will heal the sick. Father,
I praise you when I am too sick to pray for myself that
I can depend on my friends and brothers and sisters
in Christ to pray the prayer of faith for me. Thank you
for raising me from my sick bed, and if there's any sin
in my life, you forgive me. Father, I praise you for the
most wonderful life in the world: a life following Jesus.

Not Death But Life

I shall not die, but live, and declare the
works of the LORD.

PSALM 118:17

I praise you, glorious Father, for your Word that
you have given us to stand on. Your works are truly
magnificent and wonderful! If the doctors tell me I
have an incurable disease and that there is nothing
they can do, I will declare your Word over my body
and know that I shall not die, but live, proclaiming your
wonderful works. Thank you, Father, for your positive
promises, which give hope to the weakest in heart.
Father, I boldly declare your works! Glory!

Sun of Righteousness

But for you who fear my name, the sun of righteousness shall rise with healing in its wings. You shall go out leaping like calves from the stall.

MALACHI 4:2, ESV

Father, I bless and praise you because there's healing in the wings of the Sun of Righteousness. I praise the blessings in His wings, and one of them is healing. Thank you for setting me free so I can leap and dance with joy! Father, no worldly joy compares with the joy I have because of the healing in those wings. I continually praise, respect, and have awe for your name because of your good promises to all of your children!

Restore Health

"I will give you back your health and heal your wounds," says the LORD.

JEREMIAH 30:17, NLT

You will restore health to me, Father! I praise you because you didn't say you would have to think about it. You simply said that you would restore health to me. Thank you that you heal me of all my wounds in my body, mind, and spirit. I rejoice because I can worship you and serve you as a whole, healthy person. Father, thank you for giving me your best promises! You are the best promise-giver and the best promise-keeper in the entire world.

Refreshment to Bones

Do not be wise in your own eyes; Fear
the LORD and turn away from evil. It will
be healing to your body and refreshment
to your bones.

PROVERBS 3:7-8, NASB

Father, I don't have to be smart in my own eyes. I
worship you. I praise you. I love you. I adore you, and
because of you, I turn entirely away from all sin and
evil. Thank you, Father, that because you taught me
this, I have health to my nerves and sinews and life-
giving blood in the marrow of my bones. Thank you
that my bones aren't dry and brittle but are moist and
pliable. I reach out and accept your gift of health! I
love you, Father!

Healthy Children

Blessed are all who fear the LORD, who walk in obedience to him. You will eat the fruit of your labor; blessings and prosperity will be yours. Your wife will be like a fruitful vine within your house; your children will be like olive shoots around your table. Yes, this will be the blessing for the man who fears the LORD.

PSALM 128:1-4, NIV

Thank you, Father, that my family and I have your blessings and we walk in obedience to your Word. I praise you for healthy children! You reward me on this earth by giving me children as strong and healthy as young olive trees. Thank you, Father, for including healthy children in your promise reward of prosperity and happiness to those who love and serve you. I love to tell my children that it's you, our Father in heaven, who blesses, protects, and prospers us! Thank you, Father!

Eyes and Ears

The eyes of those who see will not be dim,
and the ears of those who hear will listen.

ISAIAH 32:3

Father, I praise you that you have given me eyes
that see and ears that hear, for your Word says that I
have them. Because my eyes are not dim in spiritual
matters, I am not fooled by the devil's temptations.
Because my ears are not deaf in spiritual things, I am
not deceived by the devil's lies. I see and hear correctly
because you have blessed me with physical health and
spiritual discernment, and I praise you for that, Father.
You are a wonderful God, who is loving, merciful, and
powerful!

Great Physician

No evil shall befall you, nor shall any
plague come near your dwelling.

PSALM 91:10

Thank you, Father, for protecting me from all illness
and disease. Your Word promises that you won't
let any evil or plague overtake me. I thank you for
protection from colds, flu, infections, and plagues of
any kind. Father, you are my physician, and you have
the best hospitalization plan in the world, which is for
us to stay healthy! You can heal anything that befalls
me, and I love you for keeping me healthy so I don't
have to get healed! Thank you for divine health! Thank
you for that divine protection from accidents too.
Thank you for that barrier around me that protects me
from wicked tongues. Thank you for protection of *all*
kinds.

Stop the Blood

And when I passed by you and saw you struggling in your own blood, I said to you in your blood, "Live!" Yes, I said to you in your blood, "Live!"

EZEKIEL 16:6

Father, thank you for protection from hemorrhaging during childbirth or any other time. I praise and thank you because when my blood flows from me during an attack from the devil, I can stand on the rock of your Word. I know that you say, "Live," to me. Thank you for loving me so much that you want me to be healthy, whole, and protected throughout my body. I praise you, heavenly Father, when I see a brother or sister in distress or trouble from bleeding, I can use your Word and command hemorrhaging to stop. I love you, Father!

Rising of the Sun

So shall they fear the name of the LORD
from the west, and His glory from the
rising of the sun; when the enemy comes
in like a flood, the Spirit of the LORD will
lift up a standard against him.

ISAIAH 59:19

How I thank you, Father, for your constant
protection of my health and well being. Thank you
for letting me know that the enemy will try to attack
me over and over, but when he does and it seems as
though I might be swept under, your Spirit is always
there to put up a barrier against him. I praise you for
your protection, your constant care, and your loving-
kindness from the rising of the sun until it goes down.

Oh, Healer

O LORD my God, I cried out to You,
and You have healed me.

PSALM 30:2

Father, how I praise you that when my health dwindles or even seems to be gone completely, I can cry out to you and you heal me! I love you, Father, because when I get wounded in the battle of health, no matter how deep or painful those wounds are you have promised in your Word to heal me. I praise you, Father, because things that are impossible with men are possible with you! You are a God of love, truth, and victory, and I rejoice in your miraculous healing power and glorify you for it! Thank you for another month of victorious health. I continue to trust you and your loving kindness. Thank you that all the promises I've declared this month are true! Halleljuah!

OCTOBER

The Holy Spirit

October is the month of *power*! Jesus told His disciples to go and preach the gospel to every creature. Then He immediately put up a stop sign and said, "Wait!" He told them to go in the upper room and wait for the Holy Spirit because He knew they were powerless without the Holy Spirit.

The minute the disciples received the baptism of the Holy Spirit and began speaking in other tongues, they began to preach about Jesus and glorified Him. Once you have the baptism of the Holy Spirit, your focus will be on Jesus.

If you've never received the power of the Christian life, which is the baptism of the Holy Spirit, you *will*, after declaring the Word written this month on the Holy Spirit!

You Have Power!

But you shall receive power when the Holy Spirit has come upon you; and you shall be witnesses to Me in Jerusalem, and in all Judea and Samaria, and to the end of the earth.

ACTS 1:8

I have power because your wonderful Word says so! I have ability, efficiency, and might because of your Holy Spirit! I thank you that the Holy Spirit not only fills me, but is completely diffused throughout my very soul! How I praise you for completely immersing and submerging me in the power of your Holy Spirit! You have given me the boldness of a lion to speak and share the Good News at all times. I'm talking to my neighbors. I'm talking to my fellow employees. I'm talking to the people I do business with! Father, I'm so bold today. I am your witness wherever I go today.

God Is Good

If you then, being evil, know how to give good gifts to your children, how much more will your heavenly Father give the Holy Spirit to those who ask Him!

LUKE 11:13

I thank you, Father, that you never give me anything evil. I love you and praise you because everything you give to me is good. I always want to give the best to my children, and I thank you, Father, that you want to give the best to me. I'm so glad that you love me more than I could ever love a member of my family, and that you give me better gifts than I could ever hope to give my loved ones. I am loved by you and you have given me the gift of your precious Holy Spirit. Thank you that I don't have to speculate or wonder if it's good or evil. I have complete certainty that all your gifts are good because they are from you!

Filled with the Spirit

And suddenly there came a sound from heaven, as of a rushing mighty wind, and it filled the whole house where they were sitting. Then there appeared to them divided tongues, as of fire, and one sat upon each of them. And they were all filled with the Holy Spirit and began to speak with other tongues, as the Spirit gave them utterance.

ACTS 2:2-4

Heavenly Father, I love you because the rushing sound that came on the day of Pentecost came right from heaven! I thank you that it fell upon *all* of those present and that they were *all* filled with the Holy Spirit and began to speak in tongues as the Spirit gave them utterance. I thank you, Father, because you haven't changed your plan and you don't restrict the Holy Spirit to just a few, but you give it to *all* of us. Father, I praise you for loving me just as much as you loved the disciples, and for giving me the same beautiful gift of the Holy Spirit.

OCTOBER 4

On Fire

I baptize you with water for repentance,
but he who is coming after me is mightier
than I, whose sandals I am not worthy to
carry. He will baptize you with the Holy
Spirit and fire.

MATTHEW 3:11, ESV

I'm on fire, Father, and I want to keep this fire
burning! I praise you that your promises have come
down through the ages so that I could receive the
same baptism that the disciples did on the day of
Pentecost! The fire of the Holy Spirit burns out the
chaff in my life, but is a fire that cannot be put out or
burned out! I bless you and praise you because this
indwelling power enables me to live above the sin of
the world with a complete distaste for the things of
the world! Jesus, you are mighty and you baptize me
with the Holy Spirit and fire.

Walking in Him

> Walk in the Spirit, and you shall not fulfill
> the lust of the flesh.
>
> GALATIANS 5:16

I'm walking and leaping and praising God in the Spirit! Thank you, Father, for making your Word so simple for me to understand. I'm responsive to, controlled, and guided by your Holy Spirit, and I'm walking, talking, and living in the Spirit at all times. You alone empower me to do this because you enable me to look at the lust of the flesh without gratifying those desires, which are of my human nature and not of you. I don't have to listen to the devil when he talks to me, because I'm walking in the Spirit—in power and glory, overcoming the devil all the way! How I praise and love you!

His Perfect Will

In the same way, the Spirit helps us in our weakness. We do not know what we ought to pray for, but the Spirit himself intercedes for us through wordless groans. And he who searches our hearts knows the mind of the Spirit, because the Spirit intercedes for God's people in accordance with the will of God.

ROMANS 8:26-27, NIV

Father, your Spirit is helping me to pray according to your perfect will. I bless you for giving me such a beautiful prayer language with which to pray. When my burdens are great and I don't know what to say, I pray in the Spirit and He intercedes and makes intercession for me. In the Spirit I always pray in perfect harmony with your perfect will. I praise you, Father, that the Holy Spirit rushes to my aid at all times!

Soar Higher

Therefore do not be foolish, but understand what the will of the Lord is. And do not get drunk with wine, for that is debauchery, but be filled with the Spirit.

EPHESIANS 5:17-18, ESV

Father, I'm filled up all the way to the top and running over with your Spirit! I praise you for letting me be wise in your ways so I will know what your will is. Thank you for telling me not to be drunk with wine. I praise you because my spirit can now soar higher and be stimulated more with the new wine of the Spirit than it ever can on artificial means. Father, I love you for giving me power to know your will!

No Limits

But the Helper, the Holy Spirit, whom
the Father will send in My name, He will
teach you all things, and bring to your
remembrance all things that I said to you.

JOHN 14:26

Father, thank you that the Holy Spirit is the
Comforter, Counselor, Helper, Intercessor, Advocate,
Strengthener, and Standby in all situations. I thank
you that the Holy Spirit was sent to magnify Jesus. I
thank you for not limiting the Holy Spirit in teaching
me certain truths, but for sending Him to teach me all
things, and to bring *all* of what your Word says to my
remembrance. Thank you, Father, that I can trust what
the Holy Spirit brings to my mind because it is *all* good,
and *all* from you. Thank you for being so good to me!

Living Water

But whoever drinks of the water that I
shall give him will never thirst. But the
water that I shall give him will become in
him a fountain of water springing up into
everlasting life.

JOHN 4:14

I'm drinking at the springs of living water and I'm
happy! I never get parched and thirsty as long as I
continue to drink from that water. I thank you and
praise you that you are a well within my soul that
springs up into everlasting life. Father, I praise you for
taking me out of the dry years I spent with the devil,
and you put me where I shall never thirst again. Thank
you for that well of water, which is constantly welling
up, flowing, and bubbling within me unto eternal life.

OCTOBER 10

Forever and Ever

And I will pray the Father, and He will give
you another Helper, that He may abide
with you forever.

JOHN 14:16

Father, I love you, I love you, I love you for giving
me another Helper. Even more than that, Father, I
praise you because you have promised that He will
abide with me forever. I praise you and thank you that
the Holy Spirit is abiding in me right now, helping,
comforting, and accompanying me wherever I go. I
praise you, Father, that the Holy Spirit is the Spirit of
Truth. I receive your truth, which is alive in my heart
and guiding my every step!

A Constant Reminder

But when the Helper comes, whom I shall send to you from the Father, the Spirit of truth who proceeds from the Father, He will testify of Me.

JOHN 15:26

Thank you, Father, that the Holy Spirit testifies to me about Jesus. I praise you that the Holy Spirit is the Spirit of Truth who rightly divides that which is the true from the false. I can always depend on the Holy Spirit to reveal the truth to me in all situations in the world, and also in your Word. I praise you, Father, that the Holy Spirit comes from you and not from the devil. I praise you, Jesus, that the Holy Spirit is constantly reminding me at all times of you, your love for me, your sacrifice, and your cleansing power. I thank you that the Holy Spirit is also the Counselor, Helper, Advocate, Intercessor, and Strengthener!

OCTOBER 12

No Restrictions

And afterward, I will pour out my Spirit
on all people. Your sons and daughters
will prophesy, your old men will dream
dreams, your young men will see visions.

JOEL 2:28, NIV

Father, I praise you that you are pouring out your
Spirit upon all flesh. I praise you that this includes me
and I thank you for pouring it all over me. Thank you
for giving us the ability to dream dreams, have visions,
and prophesy. I thank you and praise you, Father,
because your Spirit is a blessing to me more than ever
before. I praise you that you didn't restrict your Holy
Spirit to some, but that you freely give to all who ask.
So I ask, fill me with your Spirit afresh today.

Overcoming Evil

Therefore, brethren, we are debtors—not
to the flesh, to live according to the flesh.
For if you live according to the flesh you
will die; but if by the Spirit you put to
death the deeds of the body,
you will live.

ROMANS 8:12-13

Father, I thank you that I am not a debtor to the
flesh, and therefore I don't have to live after the
lust of the flesh. I thank you and praise you, Father,
that through the power of the Spirit, I am constantly
putting to death the evil deeds prompted by the flesh
so that I may live! I thank you that it gets easier every
day for me to turn from my carnal nature. I am putting
to death the evil deeds through the power of the Holy
Spirit.

Much Fruit

But the fruit of the Spirit is love, joy,
peace, longsuffering, kindness, goodness,
faithfulness, gentleness, self-control.
Against such there is no law.

GALATIANS 5:22-23

I rejoice and praise you, Father, for your love in my heart. The fruit of the Spirit is abundant in my life and you give me what I have not had before. I can love the unlovely! I am running over with joy and peace and longsuffering. I praise you for gentleness, goodness, and faith. I thank you for meekness and self-control. I love you for giving me not just one of the fruits of the Spirit, but *all* of them! The fruit of your Spirit is abundant in my life.

Children of God

For as many as are led by the Spirit of God, these are sons of God. For you did not receive the spirit of bondage again to fear, but you received the Spirit of adoption by whom we cry out, "Abba, Father."

ROMANS 8:14-15

I am a child of God! Father, I love you for leading me by your Spirit and for making me your child! I praise you for your Word, which assures me that I won't be left out. You say *as many as are led*, and not just a selected few, are the children of God. Thank you that I'm not caught up in slavery to fear, but instead I've been adopted into your very own family! I rejoice and thank you for the presence and power of your Holy Spirit, which enables me to do the greater things your Word promises! I have received the spirit of adoption and cry out, "Abba, Father."

God's Light

We now have this light shining in our
hearts, but we ourselves are like fragile
clay jars containing this great treasure.
This makes it clear that our great power is
from God, not from ourselves.

2 CORINTHIANS 4:7, NLT

I praise and thank you, Father, for the light inside
my physical body that is right this minute shining out
of me upon the world. The divine light of your gospel
shines so brightly that it's evident it isn't from my own
power, but yours illuminated through me. I praise
you Father, for making me a powerful floodlight that
shows the lost ones how to find you! I rejoice because
the whole world can see that the grandeur and
exceeding greatness of power and glory are yours!

Mighty Power of God

Since you seek a proof of Christ speaking in me, who is not weak toward you, but mighty in you. For though He was crucified in weakness, yet He lives by the power of God. For we also are weak in Him, but we shall live with Him by the power of God toward you.

2 CORINTHIANS 13:3-4

All of God's power is mine! Heavenly Father, how I praise you that Jesus is powerful within me. I thank you that His human body died on a cross but He was resurrected, and that He now lives by the mighty power of your Spirit. I thank you that even when we are weak in our bodies, we have your power to use to make our lives victorious at all times! Thank you, Father, for this divine privilege.

OCTOBER 18

Beyond Man

For to us God revealed them through the Spirit; for the Spirit searches all things, even the depths of God.

1 CORINTHIANS 2:10, NASB

Father, I thank you that you have revealed the secrets of the universe to us by and through your Holy Spirit. I praise you that the Spirit searches everything completely, thoroughly, effectually, wholly, and in every respect. You have made all of the things that are beyond man's scrutiny and investigation available to me! I praise you, Father, that because I have the mind of Christ, these deep truths are available to me!

A Spiritual Woman

The natural person does not accept the things of the Spirit of God, for they are folly to him, and he is not able to understand them because they are spiritually discerned. The spiritual person judges all things, but is himself to be judged by no one.

1 CORINTHIANS 2:14-15, ESV

I am not a natural or unspiritual woman, Father! I am a spiritual person who can receive *all* of the wonderful things from the Spirit. I welcome and accept the wonderful gifts and teachings of the Holy Spirit. Father, you let me investigate and appraise all things because I am a spiritual woman—because your Word says so! I praise you, Father, that even though I judge all things and all situations, I am judged by no one!

Sing with the Spirit

What is the conclusion then? I will pray with the spirit, and I will also pray with the understanding. I will sing with the spirit, and I will also sing with the understanding.

1 CORINTHIANS 14:15

Father, I thank you that I can pray and praise you with my mind and understanding, and I can also pray and praise you with my spirit through the power of the Holy Spirit! When I have feelings in my heart that can't be expressed because they are overwhelming, you give me a special way to pray and praise you with my spirit to express those feelings! I thank you that I don't have to confine my singing to my understanding, but that my spirit can sing also!

Unknown Language

For he who speaks in a tongue does not
speak to men but to God, for no one
understands him; however, in the spirit he
speaks mysteries.

1 CORINTHIANS 14:2

Thank you, Father, that you have given me an
unknown tongue with which to praise you. This
special language is a private, personal, distinctive, and
unique communication that I have with you. Others
can't understand it, but you can, Father. I praise you
that in the spirit I can utter secret truths and hidden
things to you. Your Spirit understands my spirit and
answers! Thank you, Father, for the mysteries my
spirit converses with you. You answer my prayers even
before I utter them from my mouth.

Singing in Tongues

And the spirits of the prophets are subject
to the prophets.

1 CORINTHIANS 14:32

Father, I praise you that you give me control over
my own spirit. The Holy Spirit does not force me to
do anything I don't want to do. I thank you, Father,
that you have stored in my human body the power of
the Holy Spirit, so that I can pray in tongues any time
I want to, and I can stop praying in tongues any time
I want to. I love you for this, Father. Thank you for
the glorious privilege of singing in tongues and then
stopping whenever I choose!

Dwell in Me

Now he who keeps His commandments
abides in Him, and He in him. And by this
we know that He abides in us, by the Spirit
whom He has given us.

1 JOHN 3:24

I thank you and praise you, glorious Father, for I
know that you abide in me because of the Spirit which
you have given to me. Thank you, Father, that I don't
have to wonder or question whether or not I belong
to you because your very own Spirit within me testifies
to me that you dwell in me. You have given me this
positive proof that I am your child. I bless you, Father,
for telling me that you dwell, reside, live, stay, and
abide in me, which means you accept me. Glory to you,
Father, for such a great gift.

God's Fountain

And the Spirit and the bride say, "Come!"
And let him who hears say, "Come!"
And let him who thirsts come. Whoever
desires, let him take the water of life
freely.

REVELATION 22:17

Father, you said whoever desires may come and take
of the water of life freely. I want your living water and
I drink at the fountain of life. Thank you that your Spirit
called me; thank you that you're not stingy with the
flow of that fountain. You said that I can just drink and
drink and drink! Father, I love your living water, and I
love you for giving from a bountiful supply! My heart
is overflowing with gratitude and joy because of the
wonderful things you say in your Word. I praise you
that my soul is constantly refreshed, supported, and
strengthened by it!

Right Words

When you are brought before synagogues, rulers and authorities, do not worry about how you will defend yourselves or what you will say, for the Holy Spirit will teach you at that time what you should say.

LUKE 12:11-12, NIV

How I praise and thank you, Father, that when I run into situations where I find it difficult to speak what is on my heart and I don't know the answers, your Holy Spirit teaches me quickly and wisely exactly what I need to say! I thank you that I don't have to be anxious or worried, but that I can always depend on your beautiful Holy Spirit to teach me the right words to say under all conditions.

Overcoming Temptation

No temptation has overtaken you except such as is common to man; but God is faithful, who will not allow you to be tempted beyond what you are able, but with the temptation will also make the way of escape, that you may be able to bear it.

1 CORINTHIANS 10:13

Father, how I bless you for your Word. No enticement to sin, no matter where it comes from or where it leads to, will overcome me beyond human resistance because of your compassionate nature and understanding. I praise you because I can trust you to always provide the way out so that I can be capable, strong, and powerful to overcome whatever temptation comes my way. Father, because of your faithfulness to me, I shall be faithful to you and depend on your Word to keep me from falling into ditches that lie alongside the straight and narrow way.

A Gifted Orator

And my speech and my preaching were
not with persuasive words of human
wisdom, but in demonstration of the Spirit
and of power, that your faith should not
be in the wisdom of men but in the power
of God.

1 CORINTHIANS 2:4-5

Dear Father, I praise you that we don't have to
be gifted orators but simply ordinary people who
use your boldness to share the gospel you back up
with the power of your Holy Spirit. My faith is not in
the wisdom of men, but in the power of God. Your
power will cause people to have faith in you. I love
you, Father, for using me to further your kingdom.
Hallelujah!

Winning Side!

When the enemy comes in like a flood, the Spirit of the LORD will lift up a standard against him.

ISAIAH 59:19

Father, when the enemy roars around like a lion, I don't have to worry because your Spirit raises up a standard against him that puts him to flight! Father, I love you beyond measure because I don't have to be afraid of the devil or the evil around me. I know at all times that your Spirit drives away the enemy. Thank you, Lord, that I'm always on the winning side! Thank you that I have victory!

God's Mighty Power

So he said to me, "This is the word of the LORD to Zerubbabel: 'Not by might nor by power, but by my Spirit,' says the LORD Almighty."

ZECHARIAH 4:6

Heavenly Father, I praise you that I don't have to be a superhero full of strength, nor a powerful individual who can shake mountains, because my battles are all won in the Spirit. I thank you, Father, that the same promise that you gave to Zerubbabel applies to me—that all things are accomplished not by might, nor by power, but by your Spirit. I rejoice, Father, because your Spirit dwells in me! I thank you, Father, that the oil of the Holy Spirit is never-ending. Hallelujah!

Words of Life

It is the Spirit who gives life; the flesh profits nothing. The words that I speak to you are spirit, and they are life.

JOHN 6:63

How I praise you, Father, that it is the Holy Spirit who quickens my mind to understand the truths of your Word and other truths spoken to me. Your words are spirit and life, and I thank you that because of your Holy Spirit, your Word is alive and living in me today! I thank you that I don't have to be dead in sin the way I was, but that I now have life in the Spirit! I know that my flesh conveys no benefit, there is no heavenly profit in it, and it is your life-giving Spirit that has made me come alive in Christ. I worship and praise you for that, Father!

God's Protection

And these signs will follow those who believe; In My name they will cast out demons; they will speak with new tongues; they will take up serpents; and if they drink anything deadly, it will by no means hurt them; they will lay hands on the sick, and they will recover.

MARK 16:17-18

I'm a believer! Father, how I praise you because you have promised that through your Holy Spirit, signs follow me because I believe! I thank you that I can use the name of Jesus and cast out devils and speak with new tongues! I thank you that nothing can harm me because your Spirit will protect me! Because of the power of your Holy Spirit, sick people recover when I lay hands on them! Hallelujah! Thank you for the signs that follow me wherever I go!

November

Praise and Thanksgiving

Let's make November a month of "thanks" giving—a time of great joy as we remember *all* the things to thank God for.

We thank God for Jesus, the rock of our salvation (2 Samuel 22:2). We thank God for salvation through the blood of Jesus Christ (Ephesians 1:7). We thank God for marriage (Matthew 19:6). We thank God for children (Psalm 127:4). We thank God for many blessings (Philippians 4:19). We thank God for grandchildren (Proverbs 17:6). We thank God for ministry (Ephesians 4:11-12). We thank God for His Word (Mark 13:31). We thank God for faith (Romans 12:3).

Let's declare these praise and thanksgiving declarations at least ten times each day so that our spirits will be soaring in the heavens every day this month.

On My Lips

I will bless the LORD at all times; His praise
shall continually be in my mouth.

PSALM 34:1

Bless the Lord, O my soul! All day long I bless you
because of your goodness to me. I bless you because
you are the magnificent Creator who put the stars in
the sky and separated the land from the sea. I bless
you because you always keep your promises, even
when fulfilling them requires miracles! I bless you,
Father, because you have lifted me out of darkness
and led me to victory. I bless you and praise you for
your praises are sweeter than honey in my mouth. I
praise you for your faithfulness to me. I praise you,
Father, because it blesses me to keep your praises
continually on my lips!

Wonderful Forever

Be glad in the LORD and rejoice, you
righteous; and shout for joy, all you
upright in heart!

PSALM 32:11

Father, I'm filled to overflowing with gladness in you!
I'm glad because my whole life is in your hands. I can't
stop rejoicing because you have made me righteous
through your glorious righteousness! You have made
me upright because your strength is everlasting! I can't
keep silent because if I did the very rocks would cry
out. I don't want to keep silent, for my heart tells me
to shout for joy! Father, I have to sing and shout for
joy because you've not only given me a wonderful day
today, but you've given me a wonderful future to look
forward to, in this life and the next!

Worthy of Praise

Let my mouth be filled with Your praise
and with Your glory all the day.

PSALM 71:8

My mouth declares your praises, Father, because
in all ways you are worthy of that praise! I honor and
rejoice in your name! Father, I really want to thank you
that mouth doesn't have to be filled with mockery,
scorn, contempt, complaints, deceit, and accusation.
I'm so filled with joy in praising you and your goodness
that the world's conversation habits don't interest me.
I praise and honor you because in all the blessings you
bring to me and to my family—love, joy, peace, health,
and prosperity—the glory belongs to you. I honor
you because you are a righteous and loving God, the
fountainhead of all blessings.

NOVEMBER 4

Lift Up Your Heart

It is good to give thanks to the LORD, to
sing praises to the Most High.

PSALM 92:1, NLT

Heavenly Father, I rejoice and give thanks to you
because you fill my life with so many good things
that I overflow with feelings of thankfulness. I praise
you, Father, and I thoroughly enjoy the abundance
of blessings you bring to me because of who you are!
How can I not be thankful for each bite of food when
I love the Provider with all my heart? It is good to give
thanks to you and sing your praises because it pleases
you and lifts up my heart to you. By thanking you, I
send you my love. By singing your praises, I send you
my love. Thank you for the joy you put in my heart.

Joyful Noise

Make a joyful shout to the LORD, all you
lands! Serve the Lord with gladness; come
before His presence with singing. Know
that the LORD, He is God; it is He who has
made us, and not we ourselves; we are His
people and the sheep of His pasture. Enter
into His gates with thanksgiving, and into
His courts with praise. Be thankful to Him,
and bless His name.

PSALM 100:1-4

Father, I'm making a joyful noise because I only want
to talk about you and to celebrate your presence in
my life with praise and thanksgiving. I serve you gladly
with all my heart, mind, body, and soul. I can't stand
in your presence without singing because you have
made me so glad to be your child! I praise you that we
can enter your gates with thanksgiving and I thank you
that we can enter your courts with praise. I bless and
praise you, heavenly Father.

He Rescued Me!

I will praise You, O LORD my God, with all my heart, and I will glorify Your name forevermore.

PSALM 86:12

I praise you, Father, with all of my heart and all of my being! I thank you because you made provision for forgiveness of my sins. You saved me from eternal death through the sacrifice of your beloved Son. You rescued me out of the miry clay to set my feet on solid rock. Father, I'm blessed to sing your praises because there is so much for which to praise you! I love you and praise you with every part of my being. I will glorify and lift up your holy name forever!

As Long as I Live

I will sing to the LORD as long as I live; I will sing praise to my God while I have my being.

PSALM 104:33

Father, I thank you for the privilege of singing to you as long as I live. Singing to you is special to me, Father, because each song is an expression of thankfulness that reaches deep inside me to present an offering of joy beyond words. When I praise you in song, I feel as though you are touching me as I sing. You are lifting me up to you on the wings of that song. Heavenly Father, I thank you for listening to my songs because they always make me feel close to you. As long as there is breath in my body, I will sing praises to you!

He Reigns!

Let the heavens rejoice, and let the earth
be glad; and let them say among the
nations, "The Lord reigns."

1 CHRONICLES 16:31

Father, the heavens are glad, the earth rejoices,
and I'm saying over and over, *the Lord reigns, the Lord
reigns, the Lord reigns, the Lord reigns*! Thank you,
Father, for the way my spirit leaps within me when I
say these wonderful words. I praise you for putting
into my heart and mouth these words that make my
soul sing: *the Lord reigns*! You are the Creator and the
Lord of all creation. I rejoice with the earth and join in
heaven's gladness because you are my Lord and you
rule over my life as well as everything else—visible
and invisible! Father, I'm overwhelmed with gratitude.
Even though you have so much to care for, you take
wonderful care of me!

Fruit of My Lips

Therefore by Him let us continually offer
the sacrifice of praise to God, that is, the
fruit of our lips, giving thanks to His name.

HEBREWS 13:15

Father, I offer the sacrifice of praise to you
continually, even though it's no sacrifice to praise
you, but a wonderful privilege. I praise you continually
because you bless me continually. You even bless me
while I'm praising you! Father, the fruit of my lips is
always good fruit in giving thanks to your name and
praising you for just being who you are. Let the fruit
of my lips send out the fruit of your Spirit: love, joy,
peace, patience, kindness, goodness, faithfulness,
gentleness, and self-control. Father, you are the God
of glory, and I love to praise you!

God's Good Things

I will praise God's name in song and glorify
him with thanksgiving. This will please
the LORD more than an ox, more than a
bull with its horns and hooves. The poor
will see and be glad—you who seek God,
may your hearts live! The LORD hears the
needy and does not despise his captive
people. Let heaven and earth praise
him, the seas and all that move in them.

PSALM 69:30-34, NIV

I praise you, Father, while I'm singing. I thank you for
all the good things in life. I praise you and thank you
for my family, my health, my life, and my salvation. My
praise pleases you and my heart is alive with gratitude.
You hear the needy and are attentive to the needs of
the captive. Father, I join my voice with all the angels
in heaven and people on earth and praise you with all
my might!

A Safe Path

Bless our God, O peoples; let the sound of his praise be heard, who has kept our soul among the living and has not let our feet slip.

PSALM 66:8-9, ESV

Heavenly Father, I bless you and I sing, sing, sing your praises! You hold my life in your hands just as you hold all creation. I bless and thank you for that. In your hands you have everything—breath, life, and our very being. Thank you, Father, for saving, guiding, teaching, and nourishing me. You've given me not just life, but everything along with it. It's a wonderful life because you constantly show me how you want me to live and what you want me to do. You light the path in front of me, you hold my feet on that path, and you guard me from stumbling. Father, I bless you for this!

Until the Sun Goes Down

From the rising of the sun to its going
down the LORD's name is to be praised.

PSALM 113:3

It's early in the morning, Father, and I'm praising
you before I even get out of bed. I praise you because
I have a warm bed to sleep in and a roof over my
head. I praise you because the sun rises each day
on your beautiful creation and because the flowers,
grass, and trees testify to your glory. I praise you for
the sunshine, for the rain, for the seasons, and for
the food you put in my mouth. I praise you for all the
wonderful things you give me to do each day and for
opportunities to tell people about you. My lips are
going to praise you this whole day long until the sun
goes down. And then, Lord, I'm going to keep praising
your name. Hallelujah!

Winning Side

Jehoshaphat stood and said, "Listen to me, Judah and people of Jerusalem! Have faith in the LORD your God and you will be upheld; have faith in his prophets and you will be successful." After consulting the people, Jehoshaphat appointed men to sing to the Lord and to praise him for the splendor of his holiness as they went out at the head of the army, saying: "Give thanks to the LORD, for his love endures forever."

2 CHRONICLES 20:20-22, NIV

Father, I praise you that I am established and am prospering. I praise you for the fantastic power that there is in praise. Thank you, Father, that when the enemies came after your children, the very moment they began to sing and praise, you caused the other armies to begin fighting among themselves, and they were destroyed! Thank you, Father, that because I am your child, I'm on the winning side at all times! Hallelujah!

Overflowing Love

For I will pour water on him who is thirsty,
and floods on the dry ground; I will pour
My Spirit on your descendants, and My
blessing on your offspring.

ISAIAH 44:3

Pour your water on me, Lord, because I'm thirsty!
I praise you that you don't give me a tiny little straw
to sip water when I'm thirsty, but you pour it all over
me. There is so much that it even soaks the dry ground
around me. Thank you that there is not only enough
for me, but also for my offspring. I thank you that
my children, and their children, are splashing in the
overflow that you've given to me. I will bless you at
all times, and your praise shall continually be in my
mouth!

Unable to Stand

The trumpeters and singers performed together in unison to praise and give thanks to the LORD. Accompanied by trumpets, cymbals, and other instruments, they raised their voices and praised the LORD with these words: "He is good! His faithful love endures forever!" At that moment a thick cloud filled the Temple of the LORD. The priests could not continue their service because of the cloud, for the glorious presence of the Lord filled the Temple of God.

2 CHRONICLES 5:13-14, NLT

Your glory surrounds praise! I praise you because the minute I begin to praise and bless you, your glory fills the temple to such an extent that at times I can't stand on my feet. Thank you, Father, that you don't reserve all the good things for heaven, but you let me have some of your glory down here! I bless you for power and majesty and glory so strong that I can't even stand up!

NOVEMBER 16

God's Shelter

Because your steadfast love is better than life, my lips will praise you. So I will bless you as long as I live; in your name I will lift up my hands.

PSALM 63:3-4, ESV

Father, I search for you and my soul thirsts for you. I rejoice in you, my God, because through the night you protect me in the shadow of your wings. My protection and success come from you alone. No enemy can reach me because of your love and kindness. Thank you for leading me to the mighty, towering rock of safety. I shall forever live in your tabernacle in the shelter of your wings. Thank you for all the blessings you reserve for those who call on your name!

Glorious Deeds

Oh, give thanks to the LORD! Call upon
His name; make known His deeds among
the peoples. Sing to Him, sing psalms to
Him; talk of all His wondrous works. Glory
in His holy name; let the hearts of those
rejoice who seek the Lord. Seek the Lord
and His strength; seek His face evermore.
Remember His marvelous works which He
has done, His wonders, and the judgments
of His mouth.

PSALM 105:1-5

Father, I sing praises to you. I talk of all your deeds
and devoutly and earnestly make them known.
Father, my heart rejoices because I seek you as my
indispensable necessity. I thank you that you are
always there. Father, I shall seek your face all the days
of my life and will remember all the wonderful and
exciting deeds you have done. Hallelujah!

Rock of Our Salvation

Oh come, let us sing to the Lord! Let us shout joyfully to the Rock of our salvation. Let us come before His presence with thanksgiving; let us shout joyfully to Him with psalms. For the LORD is the great God, and the great King above all gods.

PSALM 95:1-3

I praise you, glorious Father, and sing songs before you and make a joyful noise to you because you are the Rock of my salvation. My heart wants to glorify you! I make joyful noises to you, Father, with thanksgiving in my heart and I enter before your presence with thanksgiving and songs of praise. You do so much for me that I just want to rejoice and celebrate before you! Father, I praise and thank you because you are a great God, a great King above all kings, and you are mine!

Rescued Me

Teach me Your way, O LORD; I will walk
in Your truth; unite my heart to fear Your
name. I will praise You, O LORD my God,
with all my heart, and I will glorify Your
name forevermore. For great is Your
mercy toward me, and You have delivered
my soul from the depths of Sheol.

PSALM 86:11-13

Father, I praise you for teaching me your ways so I
can avoid the deceptions of the devil and walk in the
truth. Tell me what to do and I will do it. Tell me where
you want me to go and I will go there. Every part of
my being unites in reverence and praise to your name.
With every bit of my heart, I praise you and give glory
to you. You are so kind to me and have rescued me
from deepest hell! Father, I praise you constantly.

Jehovah Be Your Name

But let the righteous be glad; let them rejoice before God; yes, let them rejoice exceedingly. Sing to God, sing praises to His name; extol Him who rides on the clouds, by His name YAH, and rejoice before Him.

PSALM 68:3-4

Heavenly Father, I am uncompromisingly righteous because of your power, and I'm glad. I jubilantly rejoice because I worship, follow, and obey the God of glory and righteousness! Father, just praising you makes my entire spirit and soul feel merry. My mouth is filled with your praise and your honor all day long, for you are the Lord of creation, the great God over the heavens. I sing your praises because my tongue can't keep still in my mouth. I love you so much. Father, I rejoice before you—Jehovah is your name!

Clap Your Hands

Oh, clap your hands, all you peoples!
Shout to God with the voice of triumph!
For the LORD Most High is awesome; He is
a great King over all the earth.

PSALM 47:1-2

Father, I clap, clap, clap my hands and rejoice with all
my heart and all my mind. I shout triumphant praises
to you, for you are the Lord above all lords, the God
above all gods. You are awesome beyond words.
The nations rise and fall at your command. All the
presidents, kings, premiers, and other world leaders
have their power only because you allow it. Kings
and kingdoms come and go, but your reign is forever,
heavenly Father. I praise you because your power is
exercised in righteousness and love toward all your
people. Father, I thank you, praise you, and shout
praises to you because of who you are! Glory!

Victory in Jesus

Blessed be the LORD! For he has heard the
voice of my pleas for mercy. The LORD
is my strength and my shield; in him my
heart trusts, and I am helped; my heart
exults, and with my song I give thanks
to him. The LORD is the strength of his
people; he is the saving refuge of his
anointed.

PSALM 28:6-8, ESV

I bless you, Father, because you hear me whenever
I cry out to you for help. I praise you because you are
my entire strength in time of need, my impenetrable
shield in time of danger. You are with me always, and
I fear no evil, not even the devil himself! I relax and
my tensions disappear because I trust, rely on, and
confidently lean on you. Father, you never let me
down. Because I am victorious in you, my heart is filled
with joy and I sing your praises!

Everlasting Joy

I will declare Your name to My brethren; in the midst of the congregation I will praise You.

PSALM 22:22

I'll gladly praise you and talk about you to my friends and relatives, Father. You'll be there to soften their hearts and open their ears. I'll praise you as they consider your Word and praise you when they finally accept your Word. When they come to know you as I know you, Father, they'll want to praise you too! I will even stand up in front of the congregation, Father, and tell about all the wonderful things you have done. I will publicly declare my testimony in the presence of those who love you and worship you. I'll praise you in the midst of them. My heart rejoices with everlasting joy and I worship you.

Thankful Day

Then each one's praise will come from
God.

1 CORINTHIANS 4:5B

Father, I praise you that on the very special day
when I stand before you in judgment, you will examine
the secret places of my heart. At that time, praise will
be turned around and you will give to us praise and
commendation for the things I have done on earth!
Father, on that day I with thank you in person for all
the wonderful things you did for me on this earth! But
your Word also says you're going to thank *me*! I rejoice
at the thought of that wonderful day to come!

A Winner in Christ

In God I have put my trust, I will not be
afraid. What can man do to me? Vows
made to You are binding upon me, O God;
I will render praises to You.

PSALM 56:11-12

Father, I praise you and thank you because my trust
is entirely in you and not in my own strength. With you
as my fortress, I'm not going to fear what any man
can do to me. Criticism and ridicule can't harm me,
for I am shielded by your truth. Enemies can't touch
me, for you confound, confuse, and defeat them by
your strength. I rejoice that vows made to you are
binding upon me, Father. In your strength, power, and
faithfulness, my victory is assured in all circumstances!
Because I trust you with all my heart, you've made me
a winner. Father, I sing your praises!

NOVEMBER 26

Beauty of Holiness

Give unto the LORD, O you mighty ones,
give unto the LORD glory and strength.
Give unto the LORD the glory due to His
name; worship the LORD in the beauty of
holiness.

PSALM 29:1-2

Thank you, Father, that I can come before you
with praise, giving you the glory and strength you
deserve for all you have done and are doing for your
people. I glorify you, Father, for passing on to me
the inheritance of Abraham. I glorify you for giving
me your Word, so that I can find instruction and
understanding. I glorify you for my salvation and the
blessings that go with it. You are a mighty God and you
deserve all glory! I see that your holiness is beautiful
and I rejoice to worship you.

He Hears You

Sing praises to the LORD, who dwells
in Zion; Declare among the peoples
His deeds. For He who requires blood
remembers them; He does not forget the
cry of the afflicted.

PSALM 9:11-12, NASB

I praise you, Father, and sing your praises around
the world! My tongue just won't keep still, but breaks
out in songs of praise. You always hear me when I call
to you, no matter what kind of trouble I am in. I praise
you, Father, for your love and power. Your deeds, on
behalf of your people, include many miracles, signs,
and wonders. You hear and remember the cry of the
afflicted. I will tell the world about them so that your
name is glorified among all the people of the earth!

My God

I will love You, O LORD, my strength. The LORD is my rock and my fortress and my deliverer; my God, my strength, in whom I will trust; my shield and the horn of my salvation, my stronghold. I will call upon the LORD, who is worthy to be praised; so shall I be saved from my enemies.

PSALM 18:1-3

How I love you, heavenly Father, because of all the tremendous things you have done for me. I praise you because you provide all that I need for my life. You are my rock, for I stand on the truth of your Word. You are my fortress, for I am safe in you. You are my strength, for I am victorious in you. You are my high tower, for I have wisdom in you. You are my deliverer, my salvation, and my God. Without you, I would be lost in sin and darkness. I praise you, Father, for saving me from my enemies and lifting me into your marvelous light.

Song and Dance

> Let them praise His name with the dance;
> let them sing praises to Him with the
> timbrel and harp.
>
> PSALM 149:3

Father, I praise you with my dancing. I praise you for creating dancing as a form of worship to you. Sometimes, Father, I get so filled with rejoicing in you and your music, I just have to clap my hands and move my feet! You love to hear my voice and see me dance before you. I sing your praises while I dance. I use instruments to praise you even more and glorify your name!

Joyful Sounds

Praise Him with the timbrel and dance;
praise Him with stringed instruments
and flutes! Praise Him with loud cymbals;
praise Him with high sounding cymbals!
Let everything that has breath praise the
LORD.

PSALM 150:4-6

   I praise you, glorious Father, with everything I have
that makes noise because your Word tells me to make
a joyful noise to you. Father, I clap my hands, sing, and
stomp my feet, just because I want to put everything
I've got into worshiping and praising you! I praise
you with musical instruments. If can't play one, I will
bang two of my kitchen pan lids together to sound
like cymbals! As long as I have breath, I'll continue to
praise you! Thank you for another wonderful month!

December

Salvation

Salvation always begins with Jesus. We pray as you make these declarations this month, your salvation will become more real and personal to you than it ever has been before. May the Holy Spirit make you powerfully aware of the sacrifice of Jesus on your behalf as you rejoice in the God of your salvation!

Children of God

But as many as received Him, to them He
gave the right to become children of God,
to those who believe in His name.

JOHN 1:12

I received Jesus, and you received me! Father, I
thank you that because I accepted Jesus as my Savior
and Lord, you gave me the right, privilege, and power
to become your child. Because I believe in Jesus' name,
I am restored to the fullness of your love, which is
much greater than the love I have for my own children.
I thank you and praise you that the gates of heaven
have been opened to me because you sent your own
Son to call me to my eternal inheritance of everlasting
life! I love you and worship you because you don't
care what I used to be; you only see me for what I am
today, *your child*! Hallelujah, Father, how I praise you
for that wonderful blessing!

Born Again

Jesus answered him, "Truly, truly, I
say to you, unless one is born again he
cannot see the kingdom of God."

JOHN 3:3, ESV

Thank you, Father, for sending your Son to show
me the kingdom of heaven. I'm rejoicing because
I've been born again of the Spirit and I praise you for
making the truth so simple for me. Father, I love you
because you didn't set up a complicated test I had to
pass to get into your kingdom. You simply said I must
be born again! Thank you, Father, for opening the
windows of heaven to me! Thank you that because I
have been born again, I will see your kingdom!

Truth and Life

Jesus answered, "I am the way and the truth and the life. No one comes to the Father except through me."

JOHN 14:6, NIV

I praise you, Father, that your Word makes the way to salvation and eternal life so clear and uncompromisingly direct. Jesus said there was no other way to come to you except through Him. I praise you, Father, that I'm not wasting time searching for the way into heaven. I've knocked on the door and Jesus opened it for me! Thank you, Father, for the truth your Son brought me and for the life I have because He lives in me! I rejoice that Jesus is *the* way, *the* truth and *the* life! Thank you, Father! Thank you, Jesus!

All Fall Short

For all have sinned and fall short
of the glory of God.

ROMANS 3:23

Thank you, Father, that your Word tells me *all* have sinned and fall short of the glory of God. You didn't leave any room for arguing about whether I'm good enough to get into heaven the way I am. I praise you for making it clear that the law can't save me and that good works can't save me. Nothing I do on my own can save me. All have sinned, including me. Thank you, Father, that you have given me your Word so that I know what to do about my sins and be restored to you. Thank you, Jesus, that *all* I did to be spiritually born was to confess that I have sinned, ask God to forgive my sins, and ask you to come into my life. I was then born again!

DECEMBER 5

Wages of Sin

For the wages of sin is death, but the gift
of God is eternal life in Christ Jesus our
Lord.

ROMANS 6:23

Heavenly Father, I praise and thank you for the most
precious gift on earth, the gift of salvation! I thank you
for showing me that the wages of sin in my life are
death. I didn't have your life flowing in me and I was
doomed to be tormented in hell. Thank you, Father,
for sending your wonderful Son, Jesus, to turn my life
around! Thank you for snatching me out of the devil's
hands and giving me a new life, overflowing with your
blessings! Thank you for the beautiful gift of eternal
life in your glorious kingdom through Jesus! Glory!

DECEMBER 6

Shed for You

For God so loved the world that He gave
His only begotten Son, that whoever
believes in Him should not perish but have
everlasting life.

JOHN 3:16

I worship and praise you, Father, because you made
the supreme sacrifice by sending your only Son to shed
His blood on the cross just for me. Thank you, Father,
for loving me so much that you were willing to let
Jesus die that I might have eternal life. I can't thank
or praise you enough for doing that. I rejoice that I
believe in your Son, Jesus, who gave His life that I
might die to my sins and live in you, to your everlasting
glory! I praise you, Father! I praise you, Jesus!

Cleansed by God

If we confess our sins, He is faithful and just to forgive us our sins and to cleanse us from all unrighteousness.

1 JOHN 1:9

Father, how I love you for your faithfulness to me! I have sinned, but because I have freely admitted and confessed my sins, I rejoice in the blessing of your forgiveness. Thank you, Father, that you have not only forgiven me, but you also have cleansed me of all unrighteousness and buried my sins in the deepest sea, never to be remembered again! Hallelujah, Father, I'm clean! I'm walking in your light and your endless love. I love you with all my heart, soul, mind, and strength. Because you are faithful to me, I'm being faithful to you. I'm blessed by the joy of life I have in you! Glory! I rejoice that you always do what your Word says!

Dining with Jesus

Behold, I stand at the door and knock.
If anyone hears My voice and opens the
door, I will come in to him and dine with
him, and he with Me.

REVELATION 3:20

How I praise you, Jesus, for that day when you knocked on the door of my heart. I am so glad that I opened it and let you in. Jesus said if I heard His voice, He would come into me and dine with me. Because I heard Him, He is living in my heart right now! Thank you, Father, that I have the wonderful privilege of dining with Jesus, for I have never been so fully nourished in my whole life as I am now. I'm blessed because Jesus lives in me, I live in Him, and the river of your living water is flowing through me. Thank you, Jesus, for the marvelous things that have happened since I opened the door to you!

Knew No Sin

For our sake he made him to be sin who knew no sin, so that in him we might become the righteousness of God.

2 CORINTHIANS 5:21

Thank you, Father, that Jesus, the sinless and spotless Lamb of God, was willing to take all the sin of the world upon His shoulders that I might receive your righteousness in Him. How I love you, Father, that you were willing to let your Son go through such a terrible ordeal for my sake. And how I love you, Jesus, because it didn't matter to you how horrible my sin was, you were willing to bear it on your innocent shoulders and take it to the cross for my salvation. Thank you for loving me more than I can possibly know in this life. I rejoice and give thanks that because I am dead to sin, I have everlasting life! Thank you for taking my sins, and in exchange, filling me up with God's goodness! I received the best end of the deal, and I love you *for* it!

My Confession

> If you confess with your mouth the Lord Jesus and believe in your heart that God has raised Him from the dead, you will be saved.
>
> ROMANS 10:9

Father, I confess that *Jesus Christ is Lord*! I believe with all my heart, all my mind, all my strength, and all my soul that you raised Him from the dead to show me the way to everlasting life! Because Jesus lives, I live! Father, these words bless my tongue and lips as I confess them, and I thank you and praise you for the love that fills my heart right this minute. Thank you, Father, that I am a new person in Jesus Christ, and because I have believed, I am saved! Hallelujah!

DECEMBER 11

Call Upon His Name

For "everyone who calls on the name of
the Lord will be saved."

ROMANS 10:13, ESV

Jesus, Jesus, Jesus! Heavenly Father, how I love
to call upon the blessed name of Jesus. I know that
because I have called upon the name of your Son, I
am saved. Thank you that I am saved from darkness
and called into your marvelous light so that I might
know the truth you that you are light, and there is no
darkness in you, at all!

DECEMBER 12

All Are Lost

For the Son of Man has come to seek and
to save that which was lost.

LUKE 19:10

How I love you, Father! I didn't have to worry and
ponder about how to find Jesus and get His attention
because you love me so much that you sent Him to
find me! I was a lost sheep and even though Jesus has
many sheep with Him in His flock, I thank you that He
came to rescue me personally! Jesus knew exactly
where to look for me because there was no way for
me to escape the darkness and confusion of any sin on
my own. Because I'm found and saved, I'm blessed in
your love! I'm lifting my loved ones up to you who are
not yet saved. I thank you that Jesus hasn't stopped
seeking and saving the lost. I rejoice in your promises
that I am safe and secure in the knowledge that as for
me and my house, we will all be saved!

DECEMBER 13

Gone

> Therefore, if anyone is in Christ, he is a new creation; old things have passed away; behold, all things have become new.
>
> 2 CORINTHIANS 5:17

Father, how I bless you that I am grafted into Jesus Christ. I am connected directly into Him, locked, fastened, attached, and joined to Him, exactly the same way a branch is connected to the vine. I've been born again! I am a new person because the life of Jesus pouring into my life has made me a fresh, new creation. Thank you, Father, that my old moral and spiritual condition is completely washed away by the blood of the Lamb. I praise you, Father, for giving me the blessing of new life! The old is gone; the new has come.

DECEMBER 14

I'm Saved!

> For with the heart one believes to
> righteousness, and with the mouth
> confession is made to salvation.
>
> ROMANS 10:10

I believe in Jesus with all my heart. I rejoice
that because Jesus lives in my heart, I am made
righteous through Him. Thank you, Father, that your
righteousness is much, much more than the justice
of this world. Your righteousness is perfect and
without error. You are a wonderful, loving Father who
cares for me. You have brought me into your perfect
righteousness. Thank you, Father, for making salvation
so simple in your Word, which says that if I believe in
my heart and confess with my mouth, I am saved. I'm
telling the whole world *I'm saved, I'm saved, I'm saved*!
Hallelujah!

Individual Plan

Jesus gave his life for our sins, just as God our Father planned, in order to rescue us from this evil world in which we live.

GALATIANS 1:4, NLT

Father, I praise and thank you that Jesus was willing to give up His life to save, sanctify, and deliver me from the sin of this world. I rejoice and thank you for rescuing me from carnal greed, desire, sin, and corruption. I want to be about your business instead of the world's business. It really excites me to know that when you made out your individual plan for my life, you placed many beautiful and wonderful things on my path. I praise you for that!

Grabbed

And you He made alive, who were dead
in trespasses and sins, in which you once
walked according to the course of this
world, according to the prince of the
power of the air, the spirit who now works
in the sons of disobedience.

EPHESIANS 2:1-2

Father, how could you have ever loved me when
I was dead in the graveyard of sin? I walked in those
paths habitually, and yet you loved me enough to stop
me from following the fashion of this world. I was
under the temptations and pull of this present day,
following the prince of darkness. But you grabbed
me out of the devil's hands and claimed me for your
very own! How I praise you that even though I was
once rebellious, unbelieving, and went against your
purposes, you quickened my spirit to see you and be
born again! Thank you!

DECEMBER 17

Passed Over

Being justified freely by His grace through the redemption that is in Christ Jesus, whom God set forth to be a propitiation by His blood, through faith, to demonstrate His righteousness, because in His forbearance God had passed over the sins that were previously committed.

ROMANS 3:24-25

Father, I fall so short of being an ideal person in your sight, and yet you declare me not guilty! I praise and thank you for your unmerited favor and mercy that you freely and graciously give to me. I thank you for the cleansing and life-giving sacrifice of the blood of your Son, Jesus, to save me from your judgment! How I bless you for passing right over all the things I did and forgiving them to give me eternal life! I shall praise you forever and forever!

Workmanship

For we are His workmanship, created in Christ Jesus for good works, which God prepared beforehand that we should walk in them.

EPHESIANS 2:10

Father, I praise you that I was created by you and born again in Jesus Christ! It doesn't matter what I look like to the world because I'm doing the job that you have always planned for me to do. Thank you, Father, that I am walking in your ways and living the good life according to the plan you had put into effect for me the moment I was born. Thank you, Father, you've given me my own special path in life! It's mine and no one else can walk it except me! I am your divine workmanship created for your glory. Hallelujah!

Beholding His Glory

And we all, with unveiled face,
beholding the glory of the Lord, are being
transformed into the same image from
one degree of glory to another. For this
comes from the Lord who is the Spirit.

2 CORINTHIANS 3:18, ESV

Father, I praise you for the miracle you did in my
life! I love you for transforming my life as I behold the
glory of the Lord through your Word, transforming
and transfiguring me ever more into your very own
image in ways that I don't have to understand, but
simply accept. Father, I'm awed and thankful that you
are changing me into ever increasing splendor and into
increasing degrees of glory through the Spirit. I rejoice
at this mystery because I am being prepared to meet
you! Glory!

Gift of Salvation

Nor is there salvation in any other, for there is no other name under heaven given among men by which we must be saved.

ACTS 4:12

I rejoice in you, Father, for you understand everything and have determined your path of salvation for the world. How I praise you that I don't have to be a genius to know that there is salvation in no other name except the name of Jesus. There is no other way I could have been saved except through that wonderful, majestic, powerful, and magnificent name of Jesus! I believe in Jesus and thank you for your marvelous gift. Hallelujah!

Bread of Life

> And Jesus said to them, "I am the bread of life. He who comes to Me shall never hunger, and he who believes in Me shall never thirst."
>
> JOHN 6:35

Heavenly Father, I love the bread of life! I praise you that I will never hunger again because every day I feast spiritually on Jesus Christ, the Bread of Life. I praise you and worship you because I'm drinking at that fountain of living water. Thank you for giving me true food and drink, for in Jesus I am nourished to receive everlasting life and uplifted to live righteously in this world. Father, I love you for making such wonderful provisions for me.

Author of Salvation

And having been perfected, He became the author of eternal salvation to all who obey Him.

HEBREWS 5:9

I thank you and love you, Father, because Jesus is the author and source of eternal salvation for each and every one of us who gives heed to your Word and obeys you. In spite of the pain you suffered by letting your only begotten Son die on the cross, you love me just as Jesus loved me by dying on that cross. I thank you because even if I'd been the only person in the world, Jesus would still have planned it this way. I love you, Father. I love you, Jesus. You are the author of eternal salvation for all who obey you.

Sent for Us

In this the love of God was manifested toward us, that God has sent His only begotten Son into the world, that we might live through Him. In this is love, not that we loved God, but that He loved us and sent His Son to be the propitiation for our sins.

1 JOHN 4:9-10

Father, your love is great! It prompted you to send your Son to be crucified, dead, and buried, until He rose again so that through Him, I might live, freed of the burdens of sin, redeemed in His blood, and restored to my inheritance of everlasting life in your heavenly kingdom. How I praise you that it was not my love for you, but your love for me that made all this possible. When there was nothing I could do to be raised from death in my sins, you sent your Son to bring me back to life. Father, I bow down before you in adoration and praise!

DECEMBER 24

As a Child

Assuredly, I say to you, unless you are
converted and become as little children,
you will by no means enter the kingdom of
heaven.

MATTHEW 18:3

How I praise you, Father, that you open the gates of
heaven to those who come to you like children with
simple, uncomplicated faith. I love you, Father, for the
teaching and instruction in your Word that lets me
understand exactly what I must do to enter into the
kingdom of heaven and abide in your glory. I come
into your kingdom humbly and gratefully. Thank you,
Father!

DECEMBER 25

Peace On Earth

"Today in the town of David a Savior has been born to you; he is the Messiah, the Lord. This will be a sign to you: You will find a baby wrapped in cloths and lying in a manger." Suddenly a great company of the heavenly host appeared with the angel, praising God and saying, "Glory to God in the highest heaven, and on earth peace to those on whom his favor rests."

LUKE 2:11-14, NIV

Father, today the world celebrates the birth of your Son. I praise you for the Good News that came out of Bethlehem over 2,000 years ago. I thank you that the same Good News is going out all over the world today, touching hearts and quickening spirits, just like it did long ago. Father, today I praise you for my salvation and I pray for the world. May kings and nations feel your precious presence on this beautiful day of days!

DECEMBER 26

Do Not Perish

Do not labor for the food which perishes,
but for the food which endures to
everlasting life, which the Son of Man will
give you, because God the Father has set
His seal on Him.

JOHN 6:27

Father, this day after Christmas may we not look at
the food that perishes or the things that pass away,
but may we work and seek after the lasting food that
continues until eternal life. Jesus, thank you for the
wonderful gift of yourself. You provide abundant life
and eternal life to me and my family. You are the gift
that keeps on giving every day throughout the year. I
give all my thanks and praise to you!

Seven Seals

And they sang a new song, saying: "You are worthy to take the scroll, and to open its seals; for You were slain, and have redeemed us to God by Your blood out of every tribe and tongue and people and nation, and have made us kings and priests to our God; and we shall reign on the earth."

REVELATION 5:9-10

Heavenly Father, I offer praise and gratitude for letting me peek into the last days through your Word. Thank you, Father, for letting me know that my Lord Jesus Christ is worthy to take the book of the seven seals and to open those seals because He alone was slain and sacrificed. By Jesus' precious blood, He purchased people from every tribe, language, and nation to serve you. You've made us a royal race of priests to our God, and we shall reign over the entire earth as kings! Father, how I praise you that you included me in, and didn't leave me out of this wonderful world of your love.

DECEMBER 28

Ears to Hear

"Most assuredly, I say to you, he who hears My word and believes in Him who sent Me has everlasting life, and shall not come into judgment, but has passed from death into life."

JOHN 5:24

My ears are open to your Word, Father! I thank you for what Jesus said, and I hear it loud and clear. I believe, trust, and cling to you, relying wholly on you, and I now possess eternal life. I will never incur the sentence of judgment, and will not come under condemnation. I have already been passed over, out of death into life. I thank you that because I believe in you through Jesus, I have the blessing of eternal, everlasting, continual, ceaseless, timeless, infinite, unending, immortal, imperishable, and deathless life! Amen!

Do You Believe?

Jesus said to her, "I am the resurrection
and the life. He who believes in Me,
though he may die, he shall live. And
whoever lives and believes in Me shall
never die. Do you believe this?"

JOHN 11:25-26

I will never die. What a glorious thought! Jesus, you
raise the dead and give them life again. I bless you that
even though this mortal body shall die, the real me
shall live and never die. I thank you for that blessed
hope. Father, I glorify you for sending Jesus to save
me, and I will forever have faith in Him, cling to Him,
and rely on Him until my very last mortal breath when
I shall take on immortality and breathe a different kind
of breath! I believe, I believe, I *believe* in you, Jesus.

To See Glory

Then Jesus said, "Did I not tell you that if you believe, you will see the glory of God?"

JOHN 11:40, NIV

I want to see your glory, Father! Jesus, I want to see your glory! I wait with excitement and anticipation for that greatest day when you've promised I shall see the glory! Thank you for equipping me and perfecting me toward that day when I will at last stand before your throne and behold your glory and see you face to face. Father, how I long for that moment when I shall see your wonderful face! I'm excited about what it will be like to walk into your presence for the first time. I'm stirred up to see your glory and grace!

DECEMBER 31

Raised Up!

No one can come to Me unless the Father
who sent Me draws him; and I will raise
him up at the last day.

JOHN 6:44

Father, I praise you for drawing me to you. As I
celebrate the end of another year, I anticipate the
day when I will be raised to spend eternity with you!
Father, I bless you for having blessed me all this year.
I praise you for your goodness, grace, mercy, divine
health, peace, prosperity, loving kindness, abundance,
your Word, your Holy Spirit, healing, the name of
Jesus, strength, freedom from fear, blessings, faith,
deliverance, and love. But most of all, I thank you for
the assurance of my salvation and eternity with you.

Your Salvation Prayer

If you have never asked Jesus into your heart, please join me for this simple prayer:

Father, I want eternal life, but I know that I have done things that are not pleasing to you. I have sinned, and I ask for your forgiveness. Cleanse me of all unrighteousness. Jesus, I open the door to my heart and invite you to come in. Take control of my entire life, and make me the person you created me to be. I thank you, Jesus, for hearing my prayer and for coming into my heart as you promised. Fill me with your Spirit and empower me to be your witness in this world.

Now confess with your mouth these beautiful words: *I'm saved, I'm saved. By God's amazing grace, I'm saved!*